MATTHEW BIBLE STUDY

DISCOVER THE LIFE AND TEACHINGS OF JESUS

40-DAY BIBLE STUDY SERIES
BOOK 12

PETER DEHAAN

Matthew Bible Study: Discover the Life and Teachings of Jesus

Copyright © 2025 by Peter DeHaan.

40-Day Bible Study Series, Book 12

Library of Congress Control Number: 2024919625

Published by Rock Rooster Books, Grand Rapids, Michigan

ISBN:

- 979-8-88809-106-7 (e-book)
- 979-8-88809-107-4 (paperback)
- 979-8-88809-108-1 (hardcover)
- 979-8-88809-109-8 (audiobook)

Credits:

- Developmental editor: Julie Harbison
- Copyeditor: Robyn Mulder
- Cover design: Fanderclai Design
- Author photo: Chelsie Jensen Photography

To Hannah

Series by Peter DeHaan

40-Day Bible Study Series takes a fresh and practical look into Scripture, book by book.

Bible Character Sketches Series celebrates people in Scripture, from the well-known to the obscure.

Holiday Celebration Bible Study Series rejoices in the holidays with Jesus.

Visiting Churches Series takes an in-person look at church practices and traditions to inform and inspire today's followers of Jesus.

Be the first to hear about Peter's new books and receive updates at PeterDeHaan.com/updates.

CONTENTS

MATTHEW

The book of Matthew, named after its author, is one of the four biographies of Jesus in the Bible. (The others are Mark, Luke, and John.) Matthew is a Jew and a disciple of Jesus, as well as a former tax collector—a profession despised by his Hebrew compatriots.

Matthew's writing focuses on Jesus's ministry, sacrificial death, and miraculous resurrection. The text is also called a gospel, which proclaims the good news of Jesus.

Writing to a Jewish audience, Matthew does much to connect Jewish history and understanding to the life of Jesus. But it's not just for Jews. It's for Gentiles too—that is, all non-Jews. Succinctly,

Matthew is written to insiders (the Hebrew people) about Jesus's embrace of outsiders (everyone else). Interestingly, as a Jew, Matthew is an insider. But as a tax collector, he's pushed to society's fringe. This makes him an insider who knows what it's like to be an outsider.

From this perspective, the Gospel of Matthew serves as a smart bridge from the Old to New Testament of the Bible. It helps us better grasp the correlation between Judaism and Christianity, a link that's strong and significant.

In this way, Matthew helps inform our faith, connecting Old Testament Judaism to New Testament Christianity. This provides us with a deeper understanding and greater appreciation of the meaning behind what we believe today as Jesus's followers.

Matthew contains some of the most familiar passages in the Bible, such as the Beatitudes (Matthew 5:3–10), the Lord's Prayer (Matthew 6:9–13), and the Great Commission (Matthew 28:18–20).

In this Bible Study, we dig into all this and more as we seek to mine valuable gems from the writing of Matthew.

[Discover more about Matthew in Matthew 9:9–11.]

DAY 1: JESUS'S FAMILY TREE
MATTHEW 1:1–17

This is the genealogy of Jesus the Messiah the son of David, the son of Abraham. (Matthew 1:1)

When we read a story, we want to be engaged right away from the opening paragraph, even from the first sentence. We don't want to wade through backstory. Instead, we want to jump right into the plot.

Yet this is not what Matthew does in his biography of Jesus. He opens with a lengthy list of Jesus's family tree. Though we may spot some familiar names, we want to skim or even skip it. We want to get to the action, which begins in verse 18.

But we shouldn't do this. Matthew has a reason

for giving us Jesus's genealogy. We must know that Jesus is a descendant of Abraham and his great grandson Judah. Even more important is seeing King David in this lengthy list. Though Jesus isn't literally David's son, as in the son of David, he is so figuratively as his descendant. Many of the promises made to Abraham and David look prophetically forward to Jesus, as Savior and King.

Aside from Abraham, Judah, and David, we see other familiar names in Jesus's genealogy. This includes Isaac, Jacob (also called Israel), and Solomon. The Bible gives us information about half of the people in Jesus's family tree, but others are obscure. Nonetheless, each one plays their part to bring about Jesus's birth. He will fulfill God's promises and accomplish God's plan to save us.

Let's give our attention, however, to four unlikely names in the list.

The first is Tamar. She is Judah's daughter-in-law, as well as the mother of two of his children, Perez and Zerah. The thought makes me squirm, but Judah and Tamar's son Perez is an ancestor of Jesus. Matthew honors all three—Judah, Tamar, and Perez—in his list.

Next is Rahab. She is a foreigner, a prostitute, and instrumental in God's people conquering the city of Jericho. The writers of the book of Hebrews celebrate her for her faith (Hebrews 11:31).

Third, we see Ruth, one of my favorite Old Testament characters. She, too, is a foreigner and not a descendant of Abraham or part of God's chosen people. Yet she pledges her commitment to her mother-in-law, to her mother-in-law's people, and, most importantly, to her mother-in-law's God (Ruth 1:16).

Ruth follows her mother-in-law's perplexing instructions when she goes to Boaz at night, uncovers his feet (which may be a euphemism for something else), and lies next to him. The Bible doesn't say what happens next, but she gets his attention, and the two marry.

Last, we see Uriah, the most unexpected entry. This is because Uriah isn't biologically part of Jesus's genealogy. Instead, his widowed wife, Bathsheba, is—though Matthew doesn't share her name. This all comes about when David has an affair with her (adultery) and has Uriah killed so he can marry her (murder).

Matthew honors Uriah by including him in this list, even though his contribution is indirect, occurring only because of his death.

Through these four people—along with several

others on this list—we see that our past and our heritage don't matter to God. Trusting and believing in him do.

Do we let our past weigh us down, or do we see ourselves as God sees us? Which of these characters gives us the most encouragement and hope?

[Discover more about Tamar in Genesis 38. Read about Uriah in 2 Samuel 11.]

DAY 2: JESUS'S ARRIVAL
MATTHEW 1:18–25

When Joseph woke up, he did what the angel of the Lord had
commanded him and took Mary home as his wife.
(Matthew 1:24)

Most people are quite familiar with Luke's beloved account of the events surrounding Jesus's birth. Luke focuses his version on Mary and gives details that don't occur elsewhere in Scripture.

In contrast, Matthew unveils the story of Jesus's arrival through his stepfather, Joseph. This lets us see the same account from a different perspective, which highlights other details that are just as important as Luke's.

Joseph is engaged to Mary, but before they consummate their union, he learns she's pregnant. What horrifying news this must be to righteous Joseph. The chaste young woman he pledged to marry doesn't appear to be so pure after all. Yet despite her apparent unfaithfulness, he still cares for her and wants to spare her from public disgrace—and possibly being stoned to death (Deuteronomy 22:22).

He considers the best approach. Yet there appear to be no suitable answers, for everyone will soon know that Mary became pregnant out of wedlock. It presents a real quandary for him.

That's when an angel of God appears to him in a dream. The angel explains that Mary was indeed faithful to him. Her pregnancy is not the result of another man's actions but is a supernatural conception through the power of the Holy Spirit.

The angel reveals that Mary will have a son. They are to name him Jesus. And this child will grow up to take away the people's sins. God's messenger even connects this unprecedented event with prophecy (Isaiah 7:14).

Knowing that the Holy Spirit impregnated Mary would be a lot to take in. It would be hard to accept. Yet the upstanding Joseph does.

When he wakes, he doesn't break their engagement. Instead, he takes Mary home to be his wife. Yet they don't consummate their marriage until after Jesus's birth.

This is a testament to Joseph's character and his faith in God. We applaud him for his obedience, even though the explanation of Mary's pregnancy seems implausible.

Joseph appears at the end of Jesus's genealogy, despite him not being biologically related. Instead, Joseph becomes the adoptive father of Jesus. In this, we see that heritage passes through adoption.

As followers of Jesus, we're adopted into God's family through him (Galatians 4:4–5). This truth should give us much to celebrate.

What can we learn from Joseph's response to the angel's message? Are we known for our faith in God and obedience to his commands?

[Discover more about being adopted into God's family in Romans 8:22–23 and Ephesians 1:4–6.]

DAY 3: TURMOIL AND TRAVEL
MATTHEW 2

When [the Magi] had gone, an angel of the Lord appeared to Joseph in a dream. "Get up," he said, "take the child and his mother and escape to Egypt. Stay there until I tell you, for Herod is going to search for the child to kill him." (Matthew 2:13)

In Matthew's story of Jesus's birth, he skips the details of the inn being full, baby Jesus sleeping in a manger, and shepherds and angels showing up. Instead, he jumps right to the part about the Magi.

They search for Jesus. When they find him, they bow before the baby and worship him. They give him three presents: gold, frankincense, and myrrh.

These gifts have tangible value, which will likely finance what happens next.

After the Magi leave, God sends his angel to Joseph in a dream. The messenger commands the three of them—Joseph, Mary, and Jesus—to leave at once and flee to Egypt. They're to stay there until they hear otherwise. This is because King Herod intends to kill baby Jesus, whom the Magi rightly identified as the King of the Jews. As the king, Herod's not about to let a baby usurp his rule. Therefore, baby Jesus must die.

Joseph, Mary, and Jesus leave that night.

They stay in Egypt until Herod's death. At last, the threat of Jesus's premature execution is over. Yes, he will die, but not yet. It is not his time.

The angel appears to Joseph again and tells him it's safe to go home. Again, Joseph obeys. He returns to the land of Israel with Mary and Jesus. Yet when Joseph hears that Herod's son is ruling in his father's place, he's reluctant to return to their hometown.

That's when he receives further instruction in a dream, warning them to not go there. Instead, they go to the region of Galilee, settling in the town of Nazareth.

These sequential events allow three disconnected geographic references to Jesus's place of origin to align.

First, the Savior will be born in Bethlehem (Micah 5:2).

Yet, he will be called out of Egypt (Hosea 11:1).

Last, he comes from Nazareth in Galilee (Isaiah 9:1–2).

In this way, Jesus can hail from Bethlehem, Egypt, and Nazareth. This all occurs because of Joseph's continued obedience to God's instructions, which come to him in dreams.

How obedient are we to God's instructions? How does God speak to us today?

[Discover other people who hear from God in dreams in Genesis 20:3, Genesis 28:12, Genesis 37:5–11, 1 Kings 3:5, Daniel 7:1, and Matthew 27:19.]

DAY 4: JOHN THE BAPTIST
MATTHEW 3

And a voice from heaven said, "This is my Son, whom I love; with him I am well pleased." (Matthew 3:17)

We now shift forward nearly three decades. John the Baptist begins his ministry to prepare the way for the Savior. Stationed at the Jordan River, he baptizes people who confess their sins and repent from wrongdoing.

This is the first time we encounter baptism in the Bible. The rite, however, may connect with the Old Testament instruction for the priests to wash themselves in the bronze basin before they ministered to God at the altar (Exodus 30:17–21). It signified a cleansing of their bodies, a purification before they approached God. John's Jewish audience would know this tradition well.

When the Pharisees, however, come to be baptized, John isn't pleased. He calls them a bunch of snakes. He doesn't see their repentance as real, with them going through the ceremony without producing fruit to confirm the sincerity of their actions. True repentance should be accompanied by a change in behavior. Otherwise, it's nothing more than a ruse.

John baptizes the people with water to show their repentance. But this is just the first step. Another will soon follow, someone far greater than John. He will baptize people with the Holy Spirit and with fire.

This also connects with the Old Testament.

Joel prophesied about the outpouring of the Holy Spirit (Joel 2:28–29). This occurs through Jesus for the early church.

Likewise, Malachi talks about the refiner's fire (Malachi 3:2–4). This references judgment: purification for God's children, and, implicitly, punishment for all others.

When Jesus asks John to baptize him, John is understandably reluctant. Since John views himself as not even worthy to carry Jesus's sandals, he wants Jesus to baptize him instead. But Jesus won't have it. He insists that John baptizing him is the proper thing to do.

It also provides for an amazing testimony about Jesus. As Jesus emerges from the water after his baptism, heaven opens and the Spirit of God descends like a dove to earth, landing on Jesus. A voice booms from heaven, "This is my Son. I love him so much. I am most pleased with him."

This shows the Holy Spirit coming to live within Jesus. It also proclaims his standing as God's Son, loved by him and affirmed for what he just did—and what he will do.

The Holy Spirit lives within all who follow Jesus. How does the Holy Spirit work in our lives? What might God say about us?

[Discover more about the Holy Spirit coming to Jesus's followers in Acts 2:1–41.]

DAY 5: MINISTRY PREPARATION
MATTHEW 4:1–11

Then Jesus was led by the Spirit into the wilderness to be tempted by the devil. (Matthew 4:1)

With the Holy Spirit now living in Jesus, we see the results of this right away. The Spirit leads Jesus into the desert. From a human standpoint, few people would willingly choose to go into a barren wilderness. Yet the Holy Spirit tells Jesus to do so, and he does. He obeys, even if it's not his preference.

After a 40-day fast, the devil comes to Jesus to tempt him. This is a wise, strategic move by Satan. Jesus is physically weak. With diminished defenses, he's vulnerable. Now is the time for the tempter to attack.

Focusing on Jesus's deep hunger, the devil suggests he turn the stones surrounding him into bread. This seems like a practical solution and is certainly within Jesus's power, as we will repeatedly see as we read through the book of Matthew.

But Jesus declines.

He won't let Satan dictate what he does, even if it's a practical solution that seems to make sense. Jesus responds with Scripture, stating that man doesn't live by bread alone but from the words of God (Deuteronomy 8:3). This passage references the manna Jesus's ancestors ate during their forty years in the desert, before they entered the land God promised to give them.

Though he failed once, the devil makes a second attempt to tempt Jesus. From the vantage of the highest point of the temple, Satan baits Jesus. This time the tempter quotes Scripture back to Jesus (Psalm 91:11–12). He says, "*If* you are the Son of God, jump, for God's angels will rescue you." The implication is that Jesus must jump to prove he is the Son of God.

Jesus, however, won't yield to Satan's ploy. The

Savior responds with a passage of his own. He's direct: "Don't test God" (Deuteronomy 6:16).

Not ready to give up, the devil tries a third time. They go to a place where they can see all the kingdoms of the world. "I'll give these all to you," Satan says, "if you'll just bow before me in worship."

It seems like a simple act to wrest from Satan the authority Adam and Eve ceded to him when they yielded to him in the garden of Eden. For Jesus, to drop to his knee—for just a moment—would be so much simpler than dying on the cross.

Yet Jesus won't have it. Again, he quotes Scripture. "Worship God as Lord and serve only him" (Deuteronomy 6:13).

The devil gives up on his efforts to distract Jesus from his mission. He leaves, and angels come to serve Jesus.

Do we know the Bible well enough to quote it when the enemy tempts us? What can we do to better hide God's Word in our hearts?

[Discover more about the Bible in Psalm 119:11 and 2 Timothy 3:16.]

DAY 6: MINISTRY LAUNCH
MATTHEW 4:12–25

"Come, follow me," Jesus said, "and I will send you out to fish for people." (Matthew 4:19)

Having fasted and withstood Satan's assaults, Jesus is now ready to begin his ministry. He moves from Nazareth to make his home base in Capernaum, around Zebulun and Naphtali. This establishes a fourth location prophesied for Jesus (Isaiah 9:1–2).

In this way, four seemingly contradictory prophecies about the Savior's place of origin all align, producing a unified account. (See "Day 3: Turmoil and Travel" for the first three locations: Bethlehem, Egypt, and Galilee.)

Jesus begins his ministry with the simple instruction: "Repent." This is because the kingdom of heaven is near (Matthew 4:17). Just as John preached repentance, so, too, does Jesus. Yet the urgency is now greater, for the kingdom of heaven draws near.

As part of his ministry, Jesus picks his first four disciples. Though he could have spread the good news about the kingdom of heaven by himself, he invites others to join him. In this way, he'll prepare them to carry on his ministry once he returns to heaven.

Jesus first taps Peter and his brother Andrew, followed by James and his brother John. They're all fishermen.

When Jesus invites Peter and Andrew to join him, he gives them a most intriguing promise. "Follow me, and you'll fish for people." In doing so, he calls them to a higher purpose. He'll turn their livelihood into a greater vision: fishing for people for Jesus.

How do the brothers respond? They immediately abandon their fishing business and follow Jesus. The brothers don't need to think about it, consult anyone else, or run it by their family. They just leave their work and go all in for Jesus.

What makes this even more remarkable is that we'll later learn that Peter is married. He has a wife to support. How is he to provide for her if he's no longer fishing? He can't. But he answers Jesus's call, making the Messiah a priority for his life. Everything else—even his wife—becomes secondary.

James and John have a similar response. They're in the fishing boat with their dad, preparing their nets to go fishing. When Jesus calls them, they also immediately respond, abandoning their father and the family fishing business.

We applaud them for their commitment to make Jesus first in their lives.

Have we made Jesus first in our lives? What have we given up to follow him?

[Discover more about being a disciple of Jesus in Luke 14:25–35.]

BONUS CONTENT: BLESSED

"Blessed are the poor in spirit, for theirs is the kingdom of heaven." (Matthew 5:3)

We'll dive into Jesus's longest recorded sermon over the next few days, but for now we'll look at his opening to this lengthy address. It's often called the Beatitudes, which means supreme blessedness or exalted happiness (Matthew 5:3–10).

Jesus gives eight examples of this supreme blessedness for us to consider.

He says:

- The poor in spirit will receive the kingdom of heaven.
- Those who mourn will receive comfort.
- The meek will inherit the earth.
- Those who crave righteousness will be filled.
- Those who show mercy will receive mercy.
- Those with pure hearts will see God.
- The peacemakers will be called God's children.
- Those persecuted for their righteousness will receive the kingdom of heaven.

Each of these eight groups will receive blessings, realizing God's supreme blessedness and enjoying exalted happiness.

Note how the first and last items provide interesting bookends to the list. Both the poor in spirit (those who view themselves as insignificant or spiritually needy) and those criticized for doing right will receive the kingdom of heaven.

Which of these eight scenarios do we most connect with? How has God blessed us?

[Discover other times of blessing in Matthew 13:16, John 20:29, and Revelation 1:3.]

DAY 7: FULFILL THE LAW
MATTHEW 5

"Do not think that I have come to abolish the Law or the Prophets; I have not come to abolish them but to fulfill them."
(Matthew 5:17)

When many people read this verse, they focus on the word *fulfill*. They assume that once Jesus fulfills the Law and the Prophets, those rules no longer apply. They think they can disregard what the Old Testament says.

This, however, is a wrong interpretation. Jesus says so. Our Savior states unequivocally that he is not abolishing the teachings of the Law and the

Prophets. He isn't replacing them nor negating them. They still apply.

In this way, we can better understand the use of the word *fulfill* to mean *extend* or *expand*. Jesus's purpose in showing us a new way to the Father is to extend the Old Testament Law and Prophets. This means they still apply to us today, but in a new, expanded way.

As Jesus continues his sermon, he shares examples of how he fulfills the Law and the Prophets.

First up is **murder**. We know murder is wrong. The Law says so, and we follow that today. Yet Jesus extends the concept. If we become angry at another, we are just as guilty.

Next, we read about **adultery**. We likewise know adultery is wrong. We see that in the Old Testament and continue to affirm it. Jesus also extends what this means. He says that if we look at another person with lust, we've already committed adultery in our hearts. From Jesus's perspective, this is just as bad as doing it with our bodies.

Then Jesus moves on to **divorce**. The Law made it easy for a man to divorce his wife. At least that's what the people in Jesus's day thought. But Jesus sets a higher standard. He clarifies that the only justification for divorce is unfaithfulness. Aside from that, he expects people to honor their marriage vows.

Fourth, Jesus talks about **revenge**. Moses stated, "an eye for an eye and a tooth for a tooth." This kept people from overreacting with excessive retaliation when wronged. A Biblical example occurs when Dinah's brothers slaughter all the men in the town because one of them raped her (Genesis 34). Lest we think too harshly of her brothers' actions, remember that they lived prior to Moses giving the people this instruction.

But Jesus goes beyond the concept of limiting our retaliation to a reciprocal response. He tells us not to take revenge at all, even to the point of doing more than requested.

The fifth example is about how we treat others. The Old Testament says we are to **love our neighbors** as much as we love ourselves. Some might infer that this gives us permission to hate our enemies. The people in the Old Testament thought so. Again, Jesus extends the concept of loving our neighbors into a command to pray for our enemies.

These show us five ways Jesus fulfills the Law and the Prophets. From this we can learn that when we encounter an Old Testament command, we shouldn't be quick to dismiss it. Instead, we should consider how Jesus wants us to fulfill that command today.

What parts of the Law have we dismissed as irrelevant? What Old Testament commands can we extend to apply to us today?

[Discover more about these five commands in Exodus 20:13, Exodus 20:14, Exodus 21:23–25, Deuteronomy 24:1, and Leviticus 19:18.]

DAY 8: WATCH YOUR MOTIVATION
MATTHEW 6:1–18

"So when you give to the needy, do not announce it with trumpets, as the hypocrites do in the synagogues and on the streets, to be honored by others. Truly I tell you, they have received their reward in full." (Matthew 6:2)

Jesus tells us to not call attention to ourselves when we do something admirable. Our goal should be to do the right thing for the person receiving it. We shouldn't proclaim our good deeds so that we receive praise for our nobility. When we make sure others will know what we did, that becomes the extent of our reward. In this case, our Heavenly Father will not esteem us further for what we did.

To illustrate this, Jesus shares three examples.

The first is giving to the poor. This could mean giving them money or giving them gifts. Some people in Jesus's day would make a spectacle of their generosity, almost to the point of throwing a parade for themselves. They would do this to receive honor from the community.

We can surmise that they didn't even care about the person who received their gift. Also, by making a public spectacle of their charity, they called attention to the neediness of the recipient. This may have debased the needy person or embarrassed them. In this way, the gift may have done more harm than good.

Second is prayer. Prayer is not a performance to impress others. Prayer is connecting with God. What the Almighty thinks about our words matters. What others think is irrelevant.

Jesus says we should pray in secret. For this reason, I'm always wary of public prayers. I'm especially concerned about people reading their prayers or reciting a liturgy.

The teacher adds that we're not to babble on with many words. There've been times when I felt my prayers were too short, so I added to them. Yet I wonder if making them longer made them any better.

Third, Jesus mentions fasting. I don't know of many people today who fast for spiritual reasons, but two thousand years ago, the Jewish people did it with legalistic adherence. When they fasted, some of them would adopt the posture of suffering. In this way, people could see their devotion through their misery. Yet the notice others paid to them was the only reward they would get. Their fasts did not connect them with the Father or have any spiritual benefit.

These are the examples Jesus gives. Yet this idea of calling attention to our acts of righteousness can occur in many other areas too. We should examine what we do and how we may wrongly call attention to ourselves.

Yes, it's wise to serve as an example to others, especially our family, but we should carefully examine our motivations each time we do something so that others will see.

When have we wrongly called attention to ourselves for the good things we have done? How can we serve as an example to others without seeking their praise?

[Discover more about our motivations in 1 Corinthians 13:1–3.]

BONUS CONTENT: THE LORD'S PRAYER

"This, then, is how you should pray: 'Our Father . . .'"
(Matthew 6:9)

W hen Jesus teaches his disciples how to pray, he gives them a concise example. These verses may comprise the most well-known and oft-recited passage in the Bible.

In the NIV, this prayer is only fifty-three words long, sixty-six words if we include the additional text at the end that isn't found in all manuscripts. Its brevity reflects what Jesus says just a few verses before, to not babble on with many words.

It's short. It's to the point. Jesus doesn't add any

fluff. This makes it easy to memorize and easy to recite.

It's commonly called "The Lord's Prayer." Others refer to it as the "Our Father" after its opening phrase. In either case, better names might be "The Disciples' Prayer" or "The People's Prayer." This is because it's a prayer for us and not our Lord, even though he taught it to us.

People often debate whether we should recite this prayer or use it as a model to guide our own communications with God. I think the answer is both.

Some situations call for the brevity of its concise wording. Other times, it provides a guide to inform thoughtful, heartfelt words that fit the moment.

In my morning time with God, I do both. First, I recite it to remind myself of its words. Then I use it as a model to guide me as I personalize it for my day. It helps me keep the words fresh and reminds me of the meaning behind those celebrated phrases.

Here are the five key concepts of this prayer (Matthew 6:9–13):

- Praise to God
- Petition for his kingdom to advance

- Request for what we need today
- Reminder to forgive others, as we have been forgiven
- Protection from temptation and evil

When is it appropriate to recite the Lord's Prayer? How can we let the principles of this prayer inform how we pray each day?

[Discover another version of this prayer in Luke 11:2–4.]

DAY 9: PREPARING FOR THE FUTURE
MATTHEW 6:19–34

"Do not store up for yourselves treasures on earth, where moths and vermin destroy, and where thieves break in and steal." (Matthew 6:19)

After talking about giving, praying, and fasting, Jesus discusses finances. Some people assert that Jesus talks more about money than anything else. I suspect this is true. Regardless, this suggests we must give the topic of money our critical consideration. We should also see wealth as a snare that could trap us.

Jesus opens by telling us to not stockpile wealth. It can be destroyed. Others can take it. We can lose it in a moment. Then we have nothing left.

Instead, we should look to place our treasure in heaven. There it will be completely safe. Nothing can destroy it. No one can steal it.

If this practical explanation isn't enough, Jesus gives us a spiritual reason too. He says that where our treasure is, our heart will follow. We can't serve two masters. We'll focus on the one and ignore the other. Therefore, we must decide. Will we serve God or money?

Jesus then plainly tells us to not worry about the future. Just as God takes care of the birds in the sky and the flowers in the field, he will take care of us.

Instead, we should seek his kingdom—and his righteousness—first. With these as our priority, he will provide the rest of what we need. We ought not concern ourselves with it.

Though we may think this is a reason to not plan, that's an overreach. As good stewards of the blessings God gives us, we should respond wisely. Yet in doing so we must put our faith in God and not in our bank account or our possessions. He matters. They don't. He's eternal. They're temporal.

When saving money, however, the question becomes how much? We should realize that we could never save enough to cover every contingency.

Therefore, we'd be foolish to try. Instead, we should make a reasonable effort to save what we'll likely need and trust God with the rest.

The key throughout all of this is to trust him with our future.

How can we best balance saving for the future and trusting God with it? In what ways can we store up treasure in heaven?

[Discover more about money in Ecclesiastes 5:10, Matthew 20:1–15, Mark 6:8, Acts 5:3–4, 1 Timothy 6:10, Hebrews 13:5, and James 4:13–17.]

DAY 10: JUDGE NOT
MATTHEW 7

"Do not judge, or you too will be judged." (Matthew 7:1)

We live today in a judgmental world. It seems everyone is quick to judge everyone else. It's easy to form an instant opinion about someone who differs from us. They may dress differently, talk differently, or act differently. They may hold a perspective contrary to ours, be it about faith, politics, or worldview.

Compared to ourselves, we view them as less than and judge them accordingly. Yet James warns us about judging others with evil intent (James 2:3–4).

Even more so, Jesus warns us against judging

others. He says that if we judge others, we'll also be judged.

We're left to wonder if this is the judgment of God or the judgment of people. The judgment of God holds more weight, yet it will occur later. The judgment of others matters less, but it's immediate. Regardless, we can lessen the sting of these judgments when we curtail our judgment of others. May it be so.

In a practical sense, judgment often comes as criticism. When we criticize others, we're in effect judging them. It's just that criticism is more socially acceptable. Though criticism may feel less weighty than judgment, we should avoid both. To help us understand the gravity of our criticism, let's frame it like Jesus's command to not judge. Then we have, "Do not criticize or you too will be criticized."

A parallel thought occurs in the Lord's Prayer. One phrase should give us pause, but we often rush past it. In it, we ask our Heavenly Father to forgive us, just as we have forgiven others.

This suggests that if we withhold forgiveness, we could be telling the Almighty he may do the same with us. Jesus's parable of the unmerciful servant illustrates this most powerfully (Matthew 18:21–35).

Yet immediately after teaching his disciples this

prayer, Jesus offers comfort. He confirms that if we forgive others, Papa will forgive us (Matthew 6:12–14).

Now let's connect judgment with unforgiveness. If we fail to forgive others, aren't we enacting judgment on them? We consider something they have said or done, viewing it as unacceptable according to our standards. We judge them as being inadequate, as falling short. Then we criticize them for it. And we seldom keep our criticism—that is, our judgment—to ourselves. We tell everyone who will listen. This means we have a critical spirit.

When we judge, criticize, and withhold forgiveness, we hurt ourselves and dishonor God. Instead, may we withhold judgment and criticism, replacing those tendencies by offering others unmerited forgiveness—just like God does for us.

If we have a critical spirit, what must we do about it? Who do we need to stop judging and forgive instead?

[Discover more about judging others in Romans 14:10, Hebrews 10:30, and James 4:11–12.]

DAY 11: MANY MIRACLES
MATTHEW 8

When evening came, many who were demon-possessed were brought to him, and he drove out the spirits with a word and healed all the sick. (Matthew 8:16)

In Jesus's Sermon on the Mount, we considered his words. Now Matthew moves from the Savior's words to his actions, sharing a string of miracles. These should fill us with awe over his power and encourage us to follow his example.

Right after Jesus concludes his lengthy message and sends the people home, a leper approaches him. He kneels before the Healer and says, "If you're willing, I believe you can restore me." The man has faith that Jesus can heal him, and Jesus does.

Next in Matthew's narrative, we encounter a centurion, a non-Jew. Since Jesus came to minister to the Hebrew people, we'd expect him to dismiss foreigners, especially one who represents his people's oppression. Yet Jesus does not. In fact, he affirms the man's faith, a confidence greater than anything he'd experienced from his own people. Then he heals the man's servant.

After that, Jesus heals Peter's mother-in-law, who's incapacitated with a fever. Later that day, he drives out demons and heals many more sick people.

Another miracle occurs when Jesus and his disciples cross the lake in a boat. A fierce storm comes up. It's violent, threatening to swamp the vessel. Yet Jesus sleeps through it. His disciples wake him and beg him to save them before they drown. Jesus rebukes them for their lack of faith and commands the wind and waves to stop. Nature obeys him. This amazes the disciples.

The last miracle in this chapter (though Matthew will share many more) is Jesus healing two demon-possessed men. Mark and Luke identify just one man in this story, but the number isn't important. It's what happens that matters. They're violent and no one can control them, posing a threat to everyone who encounters them.

Expecting Jesus to command the demons to leave the two men, the evil spirits request he allow them to enter a herd of pigs and not send them to the Abyss (Luke 8:31). He does as they request, but the pigs go berserk and rush to a lake, where they plunge in and drown.

Though we may think the demons caused the pigs to do this, killing their hosts would leave them with no physical body to inhabit. Perhaps the pigs react with hysteria over the shock of having demons inhabit them. Regardless, the pigs die, and we're left to wonder about the outcome for the demons that briefly dwelled in them.

As we consider these amazing miracles of Jesus, recall the opening paragraph above that says these accounts can encourage us to follow his example. This, however, may strike us as unlikely, if not impossible.

Yet John quotes Jesus as saying that all who believe in him will do the same things he does, and even more once he returns to his Father and sends us the Holy Spirit (John 14:12).

Do we believe we can do the same works that Jesus did? Do we believe that with him in heaven, we can do even more?

[Discover more about faith, an underlying element in many of these miracles, in Matthew 17:19–21, 1 Corinthians 13:2, and James 2:14–26.]

DAY 12: JESUS CRITICIZED
MATTHEW 9

At this, some of the teachers of the law said to themselves,
"This fellow is blaspheming!" (Matthew 9:3)

After the incident with the pigs, Jesus crosses the lake in a boat. When he arrives on the other side, some men bring to him a man who can't walk. What does Jesus do? As is often the case, he does the unexpected. He forgives the man of his sins.

The religious leaders are aghast. They criticize Jesus among themselves, saying he's blaspheming God by claiming to forgive sins, which only God can do.

Knowing this, Jesus asks them a simple question. "Is it easier to say, 'Your sins are forgiven,' or 'Get up and walk'?" To prove he can both forgive sins and heal the man, the Healer does just that. He tells the lame man to stand, pick up his mat, and go home. The man does as Jesus instructed, which amazes the crowds.

From there, Jesus invites another man to follow him. He's already called Peter, Andrew, James, and John. Now he calls Matthew. Matthew is a tax collector, a despised profession. This is because he collects taxes from his own people for the Roman government. In doing so, he works for their oppressors.

Matthew walks away from his job and follows Jesus. He invites Jesus to his house for dinner. Joining them are more tax collectors and other people the Pharisees vilify as sinners. The Pharisees criticize Jesus for spending time with them.

Yet Jesus responds by telling his detractors that these are the people who most need him. In doing so, he affirms the Pharisees for their righteousness —their adherence to the Mosaic law—while reminding them that God desires mercy more than sacrifice (Hosea 6:6).

Later that day, Jesus gives sight to a blind man and casts a demon from another man who can't talk. Again, this amazes the crowds, but it offends the Pharisees. They criticize Jesus, saying that he drives out demons only because he is the prince of demons.

Though Matthew doesn't record Jesus's response to his attackers in this passage, he does so later. At that time, Jesus again casts out a demon from a man who is blind and mute. The Pharisees once again call him the prince of demons. Then the Healer exposes the flaw in their logic, telling them that a kingdom fighting against itself cannot stand. Instead, he drives out demons by the Spirit of God.

The religious leaders first criticize Jesus for forgiving sins, next for who he spends time with, and later as being the prince of demons. Jesus deftly deals with each one, putting his critics in their place.

When have we criticized God for what he does? When have we criticized God's workers for what they do?

[Discover more about criticism in Acts 11:1–3 and 2 Corinthians 8:19–21.]

DAY 13: THE KINGDOM IS NEAR
MATTHEW 10:1–37

"Heal the sick, raise the dead, cleanse those who have leprosy, drive out demons. Freely you have received; freely give." (Matthew 10:8)

Matthew shares Jesus calling five of his twelve disciples. Now Matthew mentions the other seven by name. Jesus gathers them and gives them authority to drive out evil spirits and heal every disease and sickness. He sends them to the Jewish people with the message that "the kingdom of heaven is near."

But they aren't just to preach the good news. They're also to act. Jesus tells them to heal the sick, raise the dead, cleanse the lepers, and drive out demons.

At this point in Matthew's narrative, Jesus has modeled three of these four actions to his disciples. Though he will later do so, we've not yet seen him raise the dead. Yet he empowers his disciples to do so anyway, giving them his authority to do through his power what they couldn't do on their own.

Then he gives them other instructions for their journey: to give freely and to not take provisions. Implicitly, they're to rely on the generosity of the people they meet along the way. He tells them to seek a worthy person and stay in their house. If it's deserving, let their peace rest on it. Otherwise, keep their blessing to themselves.

If people won't listen to them, they are to leave. The disciples did what he told them to do, and they aren't responsible for the people's reaction.

Last, he tells them to be as shrewd as snakes and as innocent as doves. This is certainly a conundrum to navigate.

Telling them to cast out demons and heal the sick presents a challenge for many of his followers today. Instead of doing this literally, some today do so figuratively by providing healthcare and assistance to the people they meet. They see this as the present-day application for what Jesus told his disciples to do two thousand years ago.

Others, however, say that these instructions only apply to his twelve disciples and weren't meant for us today. Yet Jesus will later commission his eleven remaining disciples to go out into the world and tell others about him (Matthew 28:16–20). We often call this the Great Commission, and no one claims this instruction doesn't apply to us today. So why do they dismiss the earlier instructions Jesus gave to his twelve disciples?

How do we react to Jesus's command to heal the sick? How can we best navigate the words of Jesus that confuse us or seem impossible?

[Discover more about the kingdom of heaven in Matthew 7:21 and Matthew 18:1–5.]

BONUS CONTENT: DO NOT BE AFRAID

"Do not be afraid of those who kill the body but cannot kill the soul. Rather, be afraid of the One who can destroy both soul and body in hell." (Matthew 10:28)

As Jesus continues his instructions to his twelve disciples, he tells them to not fear those who will accuse them (Matthew 10:26). Then he repeats it in verse 28.

Specifically, he tells them to not fear those who could harm them physically but can't touch their soul.

There is, however, one thing to fear. They are to fear the Almighty, who has the power to destroy both soul and body, giving them eternal punishment in hell.

It's a wise perspective to not be afraid of what others can do to us but instead to live in a holy reverential fear of God's power. Yet many people do the opposite.

They fear the threat of people in front of them right now and don't fear the eternal consequences of God's judgment. But they have it backward.

Do we fear people more than God? When have we been afraid?

[Discover more about not being afraid in Acts 18:9 and Revelation 2:10.]

DAY 14: REWARD
MATTHEW 10:38–42

"Whoever welcomes a prophet as a prophet will receive a prophet's reward." (Matthew 10:41)

When your church talks about missions, how do you react? When a missionary shares their journey and wraps up their talk with a call to become a missionary, how do you feel?

Do you squirm a bit? Does it make you uncomfortable? It does me. I wonder if I should do more. Should I be doing more than writing about Jesus and supporting missionaries from afar?

Though I know I'm doing exactly what God calls me to do, I still feel guilty. But my disquiet is not coming from the Holy Spirit. I suspect it's a distraction from the enemy. I shouldn't stop doing what God has called me to do and equipped me to accomplish, only to pursue what he hasn't asked me to do and I'm not ready for.

From a practical standpoint, if everyone were a missionary, there'd be no one back home to support them. This wouldn't work out well. Just as we need missionaries, we need people who can provide financial, logistical, and prayer support for them. We also need people who can offer missionaries a place to stay when they're on sabbatical or need a break. It requires a network, with each person doing what they can.

In truth, we all have a part to play in telling others about Jesus. For some, this means going to other cultures as a vocation and their calling. For others, it means doing so locally, either as a job or as a lifestyle. And for many more, it means supporting those who take a more active role.

Jesus confirms this. He says that anyone who receives a prophet because they're a prophet will receive a prophet's reward. Anyone who receives a righteous person because they're righteous will receive a righteous person's reward. In the same way, anyone who receives a missionary because they're a missionary will receive a missionary's reward.

If God calls us to be a missionary, we should be a missionary. If he calls us to be a minister, we should become a minister. If our Lord calls us to full-time service for him, we should answer that call. And if God doesn't call us to one of these areas, we should do what we can to support those who do. This is a call that all of us can and should answer.

Are we doing what God has called us to do? What can we do —either directly or indirectly—to advance his kingdom?

[Discover more about the role we play in Jesus's church in 1 Corinthians 12:12–26 and Ephesians 4:11–13.]

DAY 15: JOHN DOUBTS
MATTHEW 11:1–19

"Are you the one who is to come, or should we expect someone else?" (Matthew 11:3)

John the Baptist came to prepare the way for the Savior. He preached for people to repent of their sins. He baptized those who responded as a public display of their repentance. Though Jesus didn't need John to baptize him, he wanted John to do so. Knowing who Jesus was, John objected. But Jesus insisted. Afterward, John—along with everyone else—heard Father God's affirmation of Jesus as the Son of God.

Later, John publicly criticizes Herod for

marrying his sister-in-law, Herodias. Herod could have repented, just like many other people. He does not. Instead, his response is to throw John in prison. This halts John's public ministry and stops his criticism of Herod.

As John languishes in prison, he has nothing to do but think. He likely recalls the prophet Isaiah's forward-looking statement that the Savior will release the prisoners (Isaiah 61:1–3). John waits for Jesus to come and do just that, to free him from his jail cell. But Jesus doesn't. In fact, there's no mention in Scripture of Jesus even visiting John while he's incarcerated.

John may wonder if he misunderstood who Jesus was and what he came to do. An inkling of doubt forms in John's mind. He sends his disciples to ask Jesus if he's the one. John's desperate to receive confirmation.

As is often the case with Jesus, he doesn't provide a direct answer. Instead, he gives a more persuasive response. He tells John's disciples to report back what's happening: the blind see, the lame walk, the lepers are cleansed, the deaf hear, and the dead rise. Through all this, the good news is proclaimed.

The evidence of Jesus's results confirms that he

is, indeed, the one. Though still imprisoned, John now has confirmation that his life's work was not in vain. He can live knowing that he accomplished what God called him to do.

In another passage, John the Baptist speaks of Jesus and simply says, "He must become greater, and I must become less (John 3:30).

This is exactly what happens. The ministry of imprisoned John becomes less, almost negligible. The ministry of Jesus becomes greater, of paramount importance: then, now, and forever more.

Yes, Jesus is the one. John knows and so do we.

Is it wrong to doubt or question our life's work like John did? What can we do to become less so that Jesus becomes more?

[Discover more about another person who doubted Jesus in John 20:24–27.]

DAY 16: RECEIVE REST
MATTHEW 11:20–30

"Come to me, all you who are weary and burdened, and I will give you rest." (Matthew 11:28)

A re you burdened? Are you weary? In today's too-busy world, many people feel burdened and weary. The enormity of day-to-day living loads them down. People long for rest, for a simpler time. They desire a break from the pressures of their lives. They want rest.

It's easy to know when our bodies need a break. We're physically tired and crave sleep. Then we hit the snooze button on our alarm one more time. We groan when we must roll out of bed in the morning. Later, as the day moves toward its end, we delay sleep to squeeze in one more thing. We fall into bed exhausted and awake the next day just as tired. Or so it seems.

Jesus promises to give us rest. Eager to receive it and full of expectation, we symbolically lift our arms to him to receive that rest.

But Jesus isn't talking about rest for our bodies. Instead, he's talking about rest for our souls. That's even more important. We all need rest for our souls, and that need is paramount.

Unlike our physical needs, it's more challenging to know what our soul needs. But our souls become burdened and weary too. Our souls need rest, but how do we find the rest our souls crave? How do we receive the rest that Jesus promises?

It's simple.

He says to take his yoke, to learn from him. He is gentle and humble. Then we will find the rest our souls require. This is because his yoke is easy, and his burden is light.

A yoke is a bar or frame designed to tow a load or carry a weight. A yoke placed between two animals makes it easier for them to pull a cart, carriage, or plow. For people, a yoke fits on their shoulders and allows them to haul a weight on either side, such as two buckets of water.

These yokes allow animals or people to accomplish more but to do so by exerting less effort. Yet a yoke can also be too much to bear. Such is the case with our souls. Our yokes can include demands society places on us, expectations from religion, and self-inflicted loads we take on with little thought. All these things can combine to burden our souls, to weigh us down with weariness.

Yet the yoke Jesus gives us is easy to bear; it's a light burden. With his yoke, we can discard the demands of society, the expectations of religion, and our self-inflicted notions.

To realize Jesus's yoke, we must learn from him. He is gentle and humble, demanding little from us.

Jesus's yoke is to follow him. It's that simple.

What have we yoked ourselves to that we must throw aside? Do we truly believe and act as though Jesus's yoke is light, as he promised?

[Discover more about yokes in Acts 15:10 and Galatians 5:1.]

DAY 17: LORD OF THE SABBATH
MATTHEW 12:1–21

"For the Son of Man is Lord of the Sabbath." (Matthew 12:8)

When we think of the Pharisees, we see a hypocritical, closed-minded people. We are quick to condemn them in this regard and rightly so. Jesus often had critical things to say about the Pharisees. Yet he affirmed them for one thing—albeit implicitly. He commended them for their righteousness (Matthew 9:11–12).

The Pharisees lived righteous lives. That is, they lived the right way, according to God's Word. They diligently followed the Old Testament Law, with its many rules and expectations. To further guide them in properly doing so, they added even more guidelines to ensure they didn't go astray.

When it came to right living, the Pharisees were the best at it. There were none more righteous than them, not then and not now.

One of the rules the Pharisees placed much emphasis on was keeping the Sabbath holy and not doing any work. When they see Jesus's disciples picking grain on the Sabbath to eat, they're understandably critical of him for allowing them to break their religious law.

Jesus counters by reminding them of when David entered God's house and ate the priests' consecrated bread. He did so without criticism or punishment. Next, Jesus calls their attention to the priests who work in the temple on the Sabbath and yet remain innocent.

He then tells them he is greater than the temple —and the laws that surround it. He is the Lord of the Sabbath. That is, he is Lord, even over the Sabbath . . . and the Law.

For all their diligence, the Pharisees had missed God's expectations with their righteous efforts. Jesus gets to the center of this issue when he quotes from Hosea, who records God's own words, "I desire mercy, not sacrifice" (Hosea 6:6). In this regard, the Pharisees had judged Jesus's disciples when they should have offered grace.

Next comes a man with a deformed hand. Seeking to trap Jesus, the Pharisees ask him if it's lawful for him to heal on the Sabbath.

Giving them a practical example, he asks them a rhetorical question. "Which of you wouldn't rescue your sheep who falls into a pit on the Sabbath? A person is much more valuable than a sheep."

Then Jesus heals the man's hand.

In this, Jesus shows them—and us—that the holy day, the day of rest, is a great day to do good.

From a practical standpoint, what does it mean that Jesus is Lord of the Sabbath? When have we let rules keep us from doing what is good?

[Discover more about righteousness in Matthew 3:13–15, Matthew 5:20, Matthew 6:1, and Matthew 6:33. Read more about the Sabbath in Mark 2:27.]

DAY 18: BLASPHEMY
MATTHEW 12:22–50

"And so I tell you, every kind of sin and slander can be forgiven, but blasphemy against the Spirit will not be forgiven." (Matthew 12:31)

Jesus says all sin can be forgiven. That's a comforting confirmation. But then he makes a curious addition. He tacks on a warning, an exception. He says that blasphemy against the Holy Spirit will not be forgiven. What does this mean? Should we be worried?

For insight into this verse, we must look at the context by examining the passage that precedes it. (See "Day 12: Jesus Criticized" for more background.)

The scenario is about the religious teachers who claim Jesus drives out demons because Beelzebul—the prince of demons—possesses him. They say this instead of giving the credit to Jesus—and implicitly the Holy Spirit who is behind his miraculous work.

In doing so, they deny the Holy Spirit's ability. They minimize or even dismiss Holy Spirit power and his work to produce signs and wonders. Given this, it worries me when I hear people argue that the evidentiary works of the Holy Spirit ended with the age of the apostles and no longer exists in our world today. In doing so, are they dismissing the Holy Spirit? Are they in danger of blasphemy against him and committing the unpardonable sin? I hope not, but we must all guard against it.

We can't know for sure what blasphemy against the Holy Spirit entails. Even so, we should exercise care to guard against committing this error. It starts when we affirm the Holy Spirit, embracing him and his role in our lives today. In doing so, we should strive to not disparage his work or minimize his power.

Some related instructions occur in this passage. Essentially, it's a call to unity. A kingdom—such as Jesus's church—divided against itself with infighting and conflict will not stand. This includes division over the role and function of the Holy Spirit. Anyone who doesn't align with Jesus and his teachings is against him. This is a person who does not build up but destroys.

What should we do if we worry that we may have spoken against the Holy Spirit? What can we do to better promote unity within Jesus's church?

[Discover more in the parallel passages in Mark 3:22–30 and Luke 12:10.]

DAY 19: THE KINGDOM OF HEAVEN
MATTHEW 13

"The kingdom of heaven is like a merchant looking for fine pearls. When he found one of great value, he went away and sold everything he had and bought it." (Matthew 13:45–46)

Matthew records Jesus talking about the kingdom of heaven thirty-one times. Given his emphasis, we'll do well to learn more about it. Jesus shares seven parables about the kingdom of heaven in Matthew 13. For three of them, he even explains the symbolism.

First, the kingdom of heaven is like a farmer sowing seed. Some seed falls along the path and the birds eat it. Other seed falls on rocky terrain. It sprouts quickly but then dies because there's no soil for it to root. More seed falls among the thorns which choke the plants. But other seed falls on good soil where it produces a large crop (Matthew 13:3–9).

Then Jesus explains what the parable means: The seed on the path represents anyone who hears Jesus's message but doesn't understand it. The evil one comes and snatches it away. The seed falling on the rocky ground refers to people who receive Jesus's message with great joy, but with no roots, it only lasts a short time. When trouble and persecution come, they fall away. The seed falling on the thorns is someone who hears about Jesus, but the worries of life and distraction of money choke it out. The seed falling on the good soil, however, refers to those who hear the word and understand it. They grow and produce a crop with up to a one-hundred-fold yield (Matthew 13:18–23).

Second, the kingdom of heaven is like a farmer (the Son of Man) who plants good seed in his field (the world). But his enemy (the devil) sneaks in and plants weeds among the wheat. When the farmer's workers discover this, they ask to pull up the weeds. But the farmer won't let them; he worries they'll uproot the wheat as well. He says to let them grow together.

At harvest time (the end of the age), the workers (angels) separate the weeds (people of the evil one) from the wheat (people of the kingdom). The workers will burn the weeds and bring the wheat into the barn, where it will shine like the sun (Matthew 13:24–30 and Matthew 13:36–43).

Third, the kingdom of heaven is like a mustard seed, which starts out small and grows into the largest plant in the garden (Matthew 13:31–32).

Fourth, the kingdom of heaven is like yeast that a woman mixes into sixty pounds of flour, working it through the dough to make it rise and become bread (Matthew 13:33).

Fifth, the kingdom of heaven is like a treasure hidden in a field. When a man discovers it, he joyfully sells all he has so he can buy the field containing the treasure (Matthew 13:44).

Sixth, the kingdom of heaven is like a pearl merchant. When he finds one of great value, he sells everything he has so he can acquire it (Matthew 13:45–46).

Seventh, the kingdom of heaven is like a net cast into a lake that catches all kinds of fish. The fisherman pulls it to shore and sorts the fish, the good from the bad. So it will be at the end times with angels separating the righteous from the wicked. The wicked will be thrown into a blazing furnace (Matthew 13:47–50).

We should carefully contemplate these seven parables, along with Jesus's other teachings about the kingdom of heaven, to better inform how we live our lives today.

Which parable about the kingdom of heaven do we most relate with? Which parable about the kingdom of heaven do we need to contemplate more fully?

[Discover more parables about the kingdom of heaven in Matthew 18:23–35, Matthew 22:1–14, and Matthew 25:1–13.]

BONUS CONTENT: TAKING OFFENSE

And they took offense at him. But Jesus said to them, "A prophet is not without honor except in his own town and in his own home." (Matthew 13:57)

After sharing seven parables to help us better understand the kingdom of heaven, Jesus travels to his hometown. He teaches the people in their synagogue. They're perplexed.

Though his wisdom and miraculous power amazes them, they still perceive him as the son of a carpenter. They know his mother and his brothers and sisters. They can't connect the Jesus they know from the past with the Jesus they see before them now.

Unable to process this, they take offense at him.

They have a fixed perception of who he is. This is a common tendency for many people. They struggle to embrace a person who leaves home and returns a better, more successful version of themselves.

This, however, doesn't surprise Jesus. He wisely tells them that only in his hometown is a prophet without honor.

Though we're aware that we can change—that we can grow and improve—we have trouble when other people do it. It's easier to continue treating them as they once were instead of adjusting our understanding of them to match who they are now.

Thankfully, God does not deal with his children this way. He puts our past behind us, even better than we can do ourselves. He celebrates who we are today and anticipates who we will become tomorrow.

May we do so for those people around us, especially our family and the friends we grew up with. May we see them as God sees them.

Who do we need to adjust our perception of? What can we do to better embrace people as who they are instead of who they were?

[Discover more about looking ahead in Luke 9:62 and Philippians 3:13–14.]

DAY 20: WALK ON WATER
MATTHEW 14

"Come," [Jesus] said. Then Peter got down out of the boat, walked on the water and came toward Jesus. (Matthew 14:29)

After Herod beheads John the Baptist, Jesus withdraws to a private place so he can be alone. But the crowds follow him. Having compassion for them, he heals them.

When evening draws near, instead of sending them away to buy food, Jesus tells his disciples to feed them. They can't. Among them, they only have five loaves of bread and two fish. But with Jesus, that's enough. He blesses what food they have and thanks God for it. Giving it to the disciples to pass out, they distribute the food. It miraculously multiplies. There are five thousand men there, plus women and children. Everyone has enough to eat, and they even have leftovers.

After the disciples collect the remaining food, Jesus sends them away in a boat, while he stays behind to dismiss the crowd. Then he ascends the mountain by himself to pray, which may be why he went there in the first place.

Just before dawn, during the fourth watch of the night, the disciples and the boat are already far from shore. The wind is against it, and the waves buffet it. Jesus heads to the boat, walking on the water.

Having never seen such a thing, the disciples cry out in fear. They wonder if they're seeing some supernatural manifestation, such as a ghost.

But Jesus tells them to calm down. "Be brave!" he says. "It's just me. Don't be afraid."

Impetuous Peter responds first, the only disciple to act. He says, "If it's really you, command me to come to you on the water."

Jesus does. Peter obeys.

Peter, too, walks on water. He heads straight

toward Jesus, full of faith that through Jesus he can do the impossible. But then the wind and waves distract him from Jesus. Realizing the peril he's in, Peter sinks. He cries out to Jesus to save him.

Jesus reaches out and catches Peter, chastising him for his doubt. The pair climb into the boat, and the wind dies down. In awe, the eleven disciples still in the boat worship Jesus. They affirm him as the Son of God.

Peter started his journey walking on water, full of faith. He succeeded . . . for a while. When he doubted, he sank. But Jesus saved him, just as he does for us when doubt assaults us.

Jesus rightly criticized Peter. The disciple let his faith to walk on water give in to doubt that he couldn't. Yet before we join Jesus in his rebuke of Peter, let's remember that if we were there, we'd likely be in the boat with the eleven other disciples without even enough faith to take the first step.

Are we more like Peter or the eleven other disciples? When Jesus tells us to do the impossible, how quick are we to obey?

[Discover more about faith in Matthew 8:10, Matthew 9:22, Matthew 15:28, and Matthew 17:20. Read about doubt in Matthew 21:21 and Matthew 28:17.]

DAY 21: TRADITIONS
MATTHEW 15:1–9

Jesus replied, "And why do you break the command of God for the sake of your tradition?" (Matthew 15:3)

We've already seen the Pharisees criticize Jesus for breaking one of their laws, working on the Sabbath ("Day 17: The Lord of the Sabbath"). In that chapter, we talked about the righteousness of the Pharisees and their steadfast devotion to keeping the Law, along with the many guidelines they developed over the centuries.

Now they return to harass Jesus again. But this time it isn't about one of the Scripture's many laws.

It's about one of their traditions. Jesus's disciples don't do the ceremonial handwashing before they eat. We find the basis for handwashing in the Old Testament Law (Exodus 30:17–21).

The Pharisees, however, expanded it to mean something far beyond the original context. They moved it from a ritual that applied to priests—before they served God at the altar—to include everyone, as something to do before every meal.

The Pharisees notice that Jesus's disciples aren't following this tradition. They criticize him for his team's noncompliance. "Why do your disciples break the elders' traditions?" the Pharisees ask. "They don't wash their hands before they eat!"

Jesus's response is direct. "Why do you place your traditions over God's commands?" He then gives them an example to make his point. It's about them not supporting their parents—as in, honor your mother and father—so they could give money to God instead.

Since Jesus highlights this, we can assume the practice occurred back then. The people used this as an excuse—a loophole—to avoid providing for their parents. In this way, they nullified God's Word so they could maintain their traditions. Jesus rightly proclaims them hypocrites.

Then the Teacher quotes from the book of Isaiah, citing the words God spoke to his prophet: "The people honor me with their words but not their hearts. They worship me using human rules" (Isaiah 29:13).

This fault, however, doesn't solely apply to the Pharisees. We continue to do this today, elevating our traditions over Scripture.

Some use their traditions to dictate what is proper to wear to church—or to the beach. Traditions can tell us what translation of the Bible to read and which to avoid. Our manmade practices dictate the appropriate posture for prayer and the "proper" way to proclaim public prayers. Other human rules tell us which school to go to and who to date. It also specifies the format of wedding ceremonies and death rituals.

Though each one of these humanly devised practices likely had good and God-honoring intentions as its basis, we've lost much of that over time as we slavishly focused on them—the manmade rules we've been taught—over what the Bible says.

What traditions might we need to reexamine? What practices should we eliminate so we can more appropriately do what God says in the Bible?

[Discover more about what to prioritize in John 5:41–42, Acts 2:42–47, Romans 12:1, and Colossians 3:1.]

DAY 22: OUT OF THE HEART
MATTHEW 15:10–39

"For out of the heart come evil thoughts—murder, adultery, sexual immorality, theft, false testimony, slander." (Matthew 15:19)

Jesus continues his rebuff of the Pharisees for their intense focus on their handwashing tradition. "You just don't get it," he says. "What you put in your mouth doesn't matter nearly as much as what comes out of it."

What's in our hearts flows from our mouths. It's much more important than how dirty our hands get. If our hearts are full of good things—God-honoring thoughts—we speak what is good and follow it up by doing what is right. If our hearts are full of bad things—evil thoughts—we will speak what is bad and follow it up by doing what is wrong.

Jesus then gives six specific examples: murder, adultery, sexual immorality, theft, false testimony, and slander. These defile a person, much more so than eating with dirty hands.

Murder is killing someone without justification or cause, often premeditated. This means it starts in our hearts. We think about it, and then there's the risk of doing it. As we covered in "Day 7: Fulfill the Law," we likewise need to guard against being angry at other people. Anger also starts in our hearts, and it spews out of our mouths.

Adultery is having sex with someone other than our spouse. This also begins in our hearts. We may then test the possibility with our words. From this flows the action of infidelity. As we also covered in Day 7, adultery is more than just the physical act. Lusting for another in our hearts is adultery too.

Sexual immorality is performing sexual acts that violate conventions. When we consider what this entails, however, we shouldn't view this from today's perspective, with its anything goes mentality. Instead, we must consider the context and look at Biblical standards—that is, expectations—found in

Scripture and from Jesus's perspective 2,000 years ago.

With the Bible as our foundation, we can understand the Scriptural view of sexual immorality as sex outside of marriage, which is between a man and a woman. That's not what society says, but it is what the Bible says. That's what counts.

Theft is taking something that doesn't belong to us. But before we commit the act, we first think about it. It starts in our heart.

False testimony is making an erroneous statement about someone else while under oath. It's perjury. It starts in our heart and comes out of our mouth.

Slander is spreading malicious statements to damage someone's reputation. Again, the impetus for this starts in our hearts.

The first step to avoiding all six of these sins is to put good things in our hearts. Then good will flow from them.

What have we put in our hearts that doesn't belong there? What should we put into our hearts to help ensure that good things flow from them?

[Discover more about our hearts in Psalms 119:10–11, 1 Peter 3:15–16, and James 3:14.]

DAY 23: PETER'S TESTIMONY
MATTHEW 16:1–20

Simon Peter answered, "You are the Messiah, the Son of the living God." (Matthew 16:16)

One day Jesus asks his disciples a question. "Who do people say the Son of Man is?" Jesus has already implicitly identified himself as the Son of Man (Matthew 9:6), so his effective question becomes, "Who do people say I am?"

The disciples reel off a bunch of answers, what they've heard among the people as they wonder about Jesus and speculate. First, they say he's John the Baptist. Next is Elijah. Others say Jeremiah. In fact, he could be any of the prophets.

Since all these people are dead, this means Jesus would be one of them in resurrected form. Of course, we know he's not someone who has come back to life. He's much more.

Now Jesus asks them a more critical question, "Who do *you* say I am?"

We might expect Peter to answer first, and he does. He says, "You are the Messiah, the Son of the living God." What a succinct response.

As the Messiah—the Christ—Jesus is the Savior sent to free the people, to liberate them. Isaiah prophesied that one would come to set them free (Isaiah 61:1). Though the people expect this will be a physical liberation from their Roman overseers, it is instead a spiritual liberation from their bondage to sin.

Next, Peter confirms Jesus as God's Son, implicitly sent from heaven to earth.

Jesus affirms Peter's astute answer, one revealed to him supernaturally by Father God. Jesus then changes the disciple's name from Simon to Peter, which means *stone* or *rock*. (Though Matthew has been calling him Peter all along, his real name is Simon; this is the first time Jesus calls him Peter.)

Having given Peter this new name, Jesus adds to

his proclamation. He says, "On this rock I will build my church."

There are different ways to interpret what Jesus means by *this rock*.

In a direct way, Jesus calls Peter the rock on which he'll build his church. This effectively elevates Peter as the disciples' leader. Though Peter has already taken a central role among the disciples and is in Jesus's inner circle—along with James and John—this makes his leadership official.

A secondary meaning is that the rock is Peter's testimony. His declaration is that Jesus is the Son of God who came to save us. On this rock-solid truth, Jesus will build his church.

Some people consider a third meaning for rock that relates to Caesarea Philippi. This, however, goes beyond the Biblical narrative to tap the historical context of a specific place in the area.

Though an interesting speculation, it's best if we focus on the first two interpretations, possibly even melding them together: Peter will lead those who follow Jesus as their Savior.

Who do you say Jesus is? How do you follow Jesus as your Savior?

[Discover more about following Jesus in Matthew 8:22, Matthew 10:38, and Matthew 19:21. We've already addressed this topic in "Day 2: Jesus's Arrival," "Day 4: John the Baptist," "Day 6: Ministry Launch," and "Day 12: Jesus Criticized," as well as in tomorrow's reading.]

DAY 24: FOLLOW JESUS
MATTHEW 16:21–28

Jesus said to his disciples, "Whoever wants to be my disciple must deny themselves and take up their cross and follow me."
(Matthew 16:24)

J esus tells his disciples what's required of them. Does this just mean the twelve of them, or might it apply to everyone? Given the verses that follow this passage, the context of this instruction relates to everyone. This includes you and me.

To be Jesus's disciple—to go all in for him—requires three things.

First, we must deny ourselves. This means making Jesus and his kingdom a priority. This means making what we want not as important as what he wants. We put Jesus first in our lives, every aspect of it. When we deny ourselves and put our Savior ahead of us, this should guide our thoughts, our speech, and our actions. As Jesus's disciples, we should banish all selfishness, self-centered attitudes, and self-seeking behavior.

Next, we encounter the confusing phrase to take up our cross. What does this mean?

For Jesus, the cross means sacrifice. For him, it was the ultimate sacrifice of giving his life for us. As Jesus's disciples, we should be willing to die for him. Few of us will be called to do that, but we must be prepared in case it should happen.

A more practical understanding is that the cross implies making less lethal sacrifices as we live a life of following Jesus in service to him. If we love Jesus, these sacrifices need not be burdensome. Instead, these are things we willingly give up to serve him and to be a part of his team.

What's critical is that we don't need to sacrifice to get Jesus's attention, earn our salvation, or merit his favor. Jesus loves us regardless of the things we do or don't do. When we sacrifice for him, we do it in response to the sacrifice he made for us. It's how we show our love to him since he already showed his love for us.

Third, we follow Jesus. For his disciples two thousand years ago, following him meant literally to go where he went. As they did this, they emulated his example and obeyed his commands. We should do the same today. The Bible—especially the books of Matthew, Mark, Luke, and John—can guide us in how to follow Jesus in the best way possible.

When we follow Jesus, we stop following other things. These only distract us from his cause, from advancing his kingdom. Some of what we give up to follow Jesus are trivial pursuits. Other considerations carry more significance, but they should still come second to our commitment to follow him.

As we've picked up our cross to follow Jesus, what sacrifices have we made? What in our lives keeps us from following him more fully?

[Discover more about the cost of following Jesus in Luke 9:57–62 and Luke 14:25–33.]

DAY 25: MUSTARD SEED FAITH
MATTHEW 17

"Truly I tell you, if you have faith as small as a mustard seed, you can say to this mountain, 'Move from here to there,' and it will move. Nothing will be impossible for you."
(Matthew 17:20)

After Jesus's transfiguration, (which we'll cover next in "Bonus Content: The Father Speaks") he, along with Peter, James, and John, come down the mountain. When they meet up with the other nine disciples waiting for them at the bottom, there's a commotion.

A man asks Jesus to heal his son who suffers from seizures. The man had first brought the lad to the disciples for healing. They tried to restore the boy to full health but failed.

Jesus rebukes his disciples for their unbelief and then rebukes the seizure-inflicting demon in the boy. The demon leaves the child, and he is instantly healed.

Later, the disciples privately ask Jesus why they couldn't drive out the demon.

Why indeed?

This is a reasonable question. They've seen Jesus do it, and they did it themselves when he sent them out to tell others about him. (See "Day 13: The Kingdom Is Near.") This time, however, they can't do it. They're confused. I am too.

Jesus tells them it's a faith issue. They don't have enough of it.

He says that with even a bit of faith—as small as a mustard seed—they can command a mountain to move, and it will move. With faith nothing is impossible.

Does he mean they can literally move a mountain? I don't know anyone with mountain-moving faith. Perhaps moving a mountain is a metaphor, with Jesus simply meaning that with faith, they can accomplish huge things, such as figuratively moving a mountain.

The topic of faith comes up often in the book of Matthew, as well as throughout the rest of the New Testament. Twenty-five of its twenty-seven books talk about faith.

In the book of Hebrews, we read that faith is having confidence in what we hope for; it's possessing the assurance about what we don't see (Hebrews 11:1). A few verses later we read that without faith it's impossible to please God (Hebrews 11:6).

At this point in our faith discussion, I'm feeling inadequate and discouraged. Perhaps you are too.

Mark's biography of Jesus includes an expanded version of this account. In it, the Healer questions the father's faith and not that of the disciples. The dad's response is immediate—and significant. "I believe," he says. "Help me overcome my unbelief!"

Jesus does just that. He then casts the evil spirit out of the boy. The boy's health is restored.

This is a powerful reminder for whenever we struggle with faith. We give whatever degree of faith we have to the situation and ask God to make up for what we lack.

How much faith do we have? What do we think about asking Jesus to help us when we doubt?

[Discover more insight in Mark's account of this story in Mark 9:14–29.]

BONUS CONTENT: THE FATHER SPEAKS

While he was still speaking, a bright cloud covered them, and a voice from the cloud said, "This is my Son, whom I love; with him I am well pleased. Listen to him!" (Matthew 17:5)

Jesus takes Peter, James, and John up a high mountain. It's just the four of them. Jesus's appearance transforms before them. His face shines as bright as the sun. His clothes glow with a pure white. As if this isn't surprising enough, Moses and Elijah appear. That's right, two men, long dead, show up and talk with Jesus.

A bright cloud covers them. From the cloud comes a voice. It's the voice of God. He says, "This is my Son, whom I love; with him I am well pleased. Listen to him!" This is Papa's second testimony about his Son.

We addressed the first testimony in "Day 4: John the Baptist," when we covered Jesus's baptism. Then, when he emerged from his water of baptism, a voice boomed from heaven. It was the Father. He said, "This is my Son, whom I love; with him, I am well pleased."

Twice God has affirmed Jesus as his beloved Son, who pleases him. This time the Father adds the instruction to listen to him. Though directed at Peter, James, and John, we can receive it as also applying to us today.

We, too, should listen to what Jesus says.

How well do we do at listening to Jesus? How well do we do at obeying what he tells us?

[Discover more about listening to Jesus in Matthew 13:9 and Revelation 3:22].

DAY 26: FORGIVING OTHERS
MATTHEW 18

Then Peter came to Jesus and asked, "Lord, how many times shall I forgive my brother or sister who sins against me? Up to seven times?" (Matthew 18:21)

Peter asks Jesus about forgiveness. He knows he needs to forgive others who wrong him (Matthew 6:15). But how much is enough? He suggests seven times, which he likely feels is most generous.

Jesus, however, has a different perspective. He usually does. Seven times is not enough. He expands the number to seventy-seven times. An alternate rendering is even more, at seventy times seven (that is, 490 times). From a practical standpoint, this is beyond counting, and that's the point. We shouldn't keep track of how many times we forgive someone who wrongs us. We should just keep forgiving them, without end. Jesus says so.

This doesn't mean, however, that we should keep allowing them to harm us, be it physically, emotionally, or financially. If there is a repeated pattern of offense against us, we should take precautions to protect ourselves. This is both practical and wise. Yet the underlying fact remains that we should continue to forgive them each time they sin against us.

Jesus then shares a parable to make his point.

Consider a king who wants to settle the debts of his servants. A man who owes him millions goes before him, unable to pay. The king orders the man and his family to be sold as slaves to repay the debt.

"Please give me more time," the man begs. "Just be patient with me, and I'll pay you back. Everything I owe. Promise."

The king feels sorry for him and cancels his debt, letting him go free.

The servant then confronts someone who owes him a few dollars and demands immediate payment. He attacks the man to show how serious he is. The other man begs for more time, but the servant refuses to offer it. Instead, he throws the man in jail until he pays back every cent.

When the king hears of this, he criticizes his servant for not extending the same forgiveness to others that he had received himself. The king reinstates the servant's debt, handing him over to be tortured until he can pay everything back.

Jesus concludes his parable by saying that this is how Father God will treat us when we don't forgive others.

Who are we withholding forgiveness from? How can we show God our appreciation for the forgiveness we received through Jesus?

[Discover more about forgiveness in Acts 2:38, Acts 10:43, and Acts 13:38. Also see "Day 10: Judge Not."]

DAY 27: DIVORCE

MATTHEW 19:1–15

"I tell you that anyone who divorces his wife, except for sexual immorality, and marries another woman commits adultery." (Matthew 19:9)

The Pharisees come to Jesus to test him. They're likely trying to trap him into saying something they can use against him, even though their prior attempts have failed.

They ask him about divorce. "Is it lawful for a man to divorce his wife for any reason?"

Jesus reminds them of the creation account, where God made us male and female (Genesis 1:27). To obey God's command to be fruitful and multiply, the man will then leave his family to unite with his wife. They become one flesh (Genesis 2:24). In this way, God joins them together, and no one should separate them.

This certainly seems to exclude divorce as an option.

Yet Moses allowed for divorce to occur. The Pharisees ask Jesus about this. The process is quite simple. A man can give his wife a certificate of divorce and send her away.

This comes from Deuteronomy 24:1, which says that if a man marries a woman who becomes displeasing to him because of something indecent about her, he can simply divorce her.

Though the wording is imprecise, Moses likely refers to a woman who is discovered to not be a virgin when she marries or one who becomes unfaithful to her husband afterward. But some men interpreted this verse as giving them permission to divorce their wife for any reason, down to the most trivial of infractions.

Jesus clarifies that Moses (not God) allowed for divorce because of men's hard hearts. That is, they lack feeling and compassion.

Jesus confirms this isn't what God intended at creation. The Teacher states plainly that a man who divorces his wife and remarries another commits adultery. The only exception is in cases of sexual immorality, which is to say infidelity.

Though this teaching about divorce specifies a man divorcing his wife, this likely reflects the culture of the day, where a woman didn't have any standing in society apart from her husband. For her, divorce was not a realistic option.

This is not the case today. Therefore, it's not wrong to interpret this verse as saying that any married person who divorces his or her spouse for any reason other than infidelity commits adultery. The essential principle is that the only time divorce is permissible is when a spouse cheats.

If you are married, stay married. If you are divorced, stay single. And if you are divorced and remarried, follow this teaching from now on.

How should we treat others who are divorced? What can we do to help married couples stay together?

[Discover more about divorce in Matthew 1:19, Matthew 5:31–32, and 1 Corinthians 7:10–16.]

DAY 28: WHO CAN BE SAVED?
MATTHEW 19:16–30

When the disciples heard this, they were greatly astonished and asked, "Who then can be saved?" (Matthew 19:25)

A man comes to Jesus and asks him what good thing he must do to get eternal life. His question reveals his heart: he wants to earn his salvation.

We will later learn we can't earn eternal life. Salvation is a gift from God that we receive by grace, through faith, and not by any work on our part (Ephesians 2:8–9).

This man, however, asks his question of Jesus prior to the Savior dying on the cross to save us. For this reason, Jesus must give the man a different response, a preliminary requirement to point him in the right direction.

Jesus tells him to keep the commandments.

Since there are hundreds of instructions in the Old Testament Law, the man asks Jesus, "Which ones?"

Jesus gives him six. The first five are don't murder, don't commit adultery, don't steal, don't give false testimony, and honor your father and mother. These are five of the Ten Commandments (Exodus 20:3–17 and Deuteronomy 5:7–21). The sixth item Jesus tells him to do is to love his neighbor as himself, something the Teacher has said on other occasions (Matthew 22:37–40).

This must fill the man with pride, because he claims to have kept all six of Jesus's requirements. Yet he knows something is still missing. "What else?" he asks.

Jesus tells him that to be perfect, he must sell all his possessions and give the proceeds to the poor. That way he'll store up treasure in heaven. Then he can come and follow Jesus.

Downcast, the man slinks away in sadness, because he has great wealth.

Jesus tells his disciples that it's quite hard for rich people to enter the kingdom of God. It's not impossible, just difficult.

This shocks them. In God's economy, wealth doesn't matter.

"Who then can be saved?" they ask.

Jesus answers, "It's impossible to do on your own, but with God everything is possible."

We'd be wrong to conclude that this passage tells us to sell everything we have to give to the poor. First, that would be trying to earn our salvation, which we already said we can't do. Second, this instruction applies only to the rich young man. For him, his money was keeping him from Jesus. His wealth was getting in his way.

When we commit to following Jesus, we may need to give up something standing in our way. It may be money, or it may be something else, such as family or possessions or our job.

What might keep us from fully committing to following Jesus? Even though we receive salvation as a gift through faith, what might we still be doing to try to earn it?

[Discover more about the proper attitude toward money in Luke 16:13, 1 Timothy 6:10, Hebrews 13:5, and James 4:13–14.]

BONUS CONTENT: THE GREAT REVERSAL

"But many who are first will be last, and many who are last will be first." (Matthew 19:30)

After Jesus tells the rich man to sell his possessions so he can follow Jesus, Peter shares what he has given up—what all the disciples have given up. "We've left everything to follow you. What about us?"

Jesus tells the disciples specifically that their reward will be sitting on twelve thrones to judge the twelve tribes of Israel.

Everyone else who gives up family or possessions for Jesus's sake will receive one hundred times as much in God's economy, along with eternal life.

"Many who are first now—or think they're first here on earth—will end up last," Jesus says. "Yet many who are last now will end up first."

God sees things differently than we do. It's the great reversal.

Will we be first or last in God's kingdom? What are we holding on to too tightly now that won't matter for eternity?

[Discover more from Jesus's parable on this in Matthew 20:1–16.]

DAY 29: SEEK TO SERVE
MATTHEW 20

"Not so with you. Instead, whoever wants to become great among you must be your servant." (Matthew 20:26)

At the end of the prior chapter in Matthew, he quotes Jesus saying that the first will be last and the last will be first. (See "Bonus Content: The Great Reversal.") Matthew then records Jesus's parable about workers in the vineyard, which communicates the same point but from a different perspective.

Neither of these passages, however, suggests that those who are last will miss out on being part of the kingdom of heaven. Instead, it's more about our status in the kingdom, which is contrary to how most people view things now.

Jesus will soon address this concept again, albeit using more specific language to give us an example of what this may mean. The context is James and John's mother coming to Jesus. She requests a place of prominence for her sons in his coming kingdom.

He tells her that this is not for him to grant but belongs to his Father.

The bold request of James and John's mother irks the other ten disciples. Jesus seizes this as a teachable moment.

He calls their attention to Gentile rulers who lord their powerful positions over the people, as well as elevated officials who wield their authority over the masses. They have power, and they use it. Why? First, because they can. Second, because it helps keep them in power.

Though Jesus could have used the Pharisees and religious leaders as an example here in his teaching, he does not. He will, however, do just that later (Matthew 23:1–12).

Instead of following the example of the Gentiles (or of the religious leaders), Jesus has a different perspective. He usually does.

He tells them that the path to greatness—of being esteemed by others—is through serving. If someone wishes to be first, they should act as a slave.

In the same way, Jesus did not come to earth so people could serve him. Instead, he came to serve them. He will soon do this in grand fashion by dying on the cross as a ransom for us. This is the highest form of service, to die for another.

Yet too many religious leaders today don't practice Jesus's words. They miss his command to serve. Instead, they expect the people under their authority to serve them. Too often they view themselves as too important to perform menial tasks. They expect others to do the hard work for them. This allows them to stand in front of the crowd to take all the credit and receive all the praise.

This is their reward—their only reward.

When have we wrongly expected others to serve us? How can we lead through serving?

[Discover more about serving others in Galatians 5:13 and 1 John 3:18.]

DAY 30: INDIGNANT RELIGION
MATTHEW 21

When the chief priests and the teachers of the law saw the wonderful things he did and the children shouting in the temple courts, "Hosanna to the Son of David," they were indignant. (Matthew 21:15)

E verywhere Jesus and his disciples go, they travel by foot. They walk. As Jesus approaches Jerusalem, we'd expect him to walk into the city like most everyone else. But Jesus isn't like everyone else.

This time he wants to ride an animal. But this won't be on a mighty steed, rather on a colt. This will fulfill the prophet's declaration that their future king will come to them riding on a colt, the foal of a donkey (Zechariah 9:9).

Since Jesus and his company don't have a colt for him to ride, they need to borrow one. He sends two disciples into the village, giving them curious instructions.

He tells them they'll find a donkey there, along with her colt. They're to take the two animals. This sounds a lot like stealing. If anyone questions them, they're to say that the Lord needs them and will return them when he's done.

The disciples do as Jesus says and bring the donkey and her colt to him. They put their coats on the young animal for Jesus to sit on. As he approaches the city, the people line the road and spread out their cloaks before him. They also cut branches from the trees to line the road. This might be the equivalent of our modern-day red-carpet treatment.

They sing their praises to him as the son of David, who comes in the Lord's name.

When he enters the city, Jesus heads straight to the temple. Once there, he drives out the merchants who are making a profit from those who come to worship. He says these sellers are making the temple into a den of robbers.

Next, the blind and lame come to him at the temple. He heals them.

The chief priests and teachers of the law—that is, the religious leaders—are indignant with Jesus, understandably so.

First, he parades into the city, basking in the people's adoration. This is something the religious leaders envy because they want it for themselves.

Next, Jesus throws the merchants out of the temple to restore right worship. The sellers are likely there with the religious leaders' approval, who may even receive payment for permission to set up their stalls.

Third, Jesus heals the blind and lame, something the religious leaders cannot do.

As a result, they're indignant with Jesus for the amazing things he did and the people's reaction to him. They criticize him. Their religious perspective keeps them from seeing God at work.

May we not repeat their error.

What part of our religion may oppose God at work? What areas of our worship do we need to reform?

[Discover more about worship in Matthew 2:11, Matthew 4:9–10, Matthew 14:33, Matthew 15:9, and Matthew 28:9.]

BONUS CONTENT: WHO WILL JOIN US IN HEAVEN?

Jesus said to them, "Truly I tell you, the tax collectors and the prostitutes are entering the kingdom of God ahead of you." (Matthew 21:31)

J esus tells his disciples a parable of two sons. The father goes to his first boy and tells him to work in the vineyard. The son says, "No." Later he changes his mind and goes. The father tells his second son the same thing. The boy says, "Yes," but he doesn't follow through.

Which son did what the father wanted? The first.

Though the second son *said* the right thing, the first son *did* the right thing.

Having shared this thought-provoking lesson, Jesus builds upon it. He says tax collectors and prostitutes are entering the kingdom of God ahead of God's chosen people.

The Jewish people despise tax collectors because they work for their Roman occupiers, extracting payment from their fellow Jews. They're viewed as traitors. The Jewish people also look down on prostitutes because they break the Old Testament laws in order to support themselves.

Yet these people are part of the kingdom of God, both in this world and the next.

Though this thought may shock us, the assortment of people who will join us in heaven shouldn't come as a surprise.

Do you identify more as God's chosen people or more akin to tax collectors and prostitutes? What do you think about spending eternity with people you ignore here on earth?

[Discover more about the kingdom of heaven in Matthew 7:21–23.]

DAY 31: THE GREATEST COMMANDMENT

MATTHEW 22

Jesus replied: "Love the Lord your God with all your heart and with all your soul and with all your mind." (Matthew 22:37)

I n the Old Testament, Moses gives the people ten commandments to follow. The first four relate to their relationship with God, and the last six relate to their relationship with others.

Besides these ten, the law contains hundreds more commands for the people to follow. Bible scholars say there are 613 such rules. Some of these instructions tell the people what they should do, while others tell the people what they should not do.

Then, to apply these directives to their everyday

life, well-meaning adherents added tens of thousands of rules to guide them. These developed and grew over the centuries.

That's a mind-numbing number of commands to follow. Who can possibly keep them all straight and consistently do what is right?

Given this, a Pharisee who is also an expert in the law approaches Jesus with a question. It's another one of their tests, trying to trap him into saying something they can use against him.

This legal expert asks Jesus to identify the greatest commandment of them all.

But the Teacher doesn't give just one. He gives two.

The first command is to love God with all our heart, all our soul, and all our mind. This means to love our Lord fully and completely. In Mark's and Luke's accounts of this exchange, they include a fourth element. It's to love God with all our strength as well (Mark 12:30 and Luke 10:27).

The second command is similar: to love others as much as we love ourselves. Note that Jesus doesn't say we need to love them more than we love ourselves, just in equal proportion. He's also not saying we need to put them first, although sometimes this may be the best way to show them our love.

The point is, we shouldn't think of ourselves more highly than others. We shouldn't elevate ourselves over them. And we shouldn't presume we're better than they are. Instead, we should love them just as much as we love ourselves.

Then Jesus adds that the law and writings of the prophets all hinge on these two commandments. This means that if we obey these two commands, the greatest commands—loving God and loving others—we effectively cover the Ten Commandments, the 613 laws, and the tens of thousands of rules about how to apply the laws.

Love God and love others is much easier to remember. Though it will probably take a lifetime to master, this doesn't mean we shouldn't attempt to do so every day for the rest of our lives.

Love God and love others.

How can we love God more fully? What should we change to love others as much as we love ourselves?

[Discover more about love in John 12:25, John 13:34–35, John 14:15, and James 2:8.]

DAY 32: MORE IMPORTANT MATTERS
MATTHEW 23

"You have neglected the more important matters of the law— justice, mercy and faithfulness." (Matthew 23:23)

As Jesus teaches the people, he warns them against hypocrisy. Specifically, he refers to the teachers of the law and Pharisees who exemplify this deception. Jesus then proclaims seven woes against these religious leaders. It's a scathing rebuke. Besides calling them hypocrites, Jesus also labels them as blind guides and snakes, as in a brood of vipers.

It's no wonder the religious leaders oppose Jesus and keep trying to trap him so they can do away with him. It's not surprising that they're planning to kill him (Matthew 12:14).

In his criticism of the religious leaders, Jesus talks about how they carefully tithe their spices but overlook more important issues. He specifically mentions justice, mercy, and faithfulness. They're so focused on the minutiae of detail in their laws that they overlook the greater matters behind it. He again calls them "blind guides" who strain out a gnat and swallow a camel.

Justice means doing what is fair and right. In a legal sense, it's impartially applying the law with equal measure to all people.

When most people clamor for justice, they feel wronged and want someone, such as a higher authority, to make it right. They seek to be elevated from their condition and have what they lost restored to them—or to receive what they never had.

Yet another aspect with justice is God's relationship to us. When we do what is wrong—that is, when we sin—we deserve punishment. Justice demands it. Yet this is not a time when we demand justice. Instead, we plead for mercy.

Mercy means enjoying compassionate treatment. It's receiving relief from our distress.

When we fall short of God's expectations, we know we deserve the death penalty. That's a blunt way of putting it, but recall that the wages of sin is death (Romans 6:23). This is when we seek God's mercy. In fact, we count on it. We see that mercy contrasts with justice.

In short, mercy is not getting the bad things we deserve. Compare this to grace, which is getting good things we don't deserve. Mercy and grace work together, showering us with God's unlimited love.

Faithfulness is a steadfast loyalty that isn't easily swayed. It's a devotion to something or someone. This may be to our job, promises we've made, or ideals we hold. We can liken this to integrity. If we're married, faithfulness finds its significance in fidelity to our spouse.

The most important area of faithfulness, however, is to God. Being faithful to him rises above all else. At the end of our life, with eternity in the balance, that's what matters.

As we seek to serve our heavenly Father, may we attend to the important matters of justice, mercy, and faithfulness.

God offers us mercy, but how well do we do at offering mercy to others? What should we do to be more faithful to God?

[Discover more about faithfulness in Romans 3:3, Galatians 5:22–23, and 3 John 1:3.]

DAY 33: BE READY
MATTHEW 24

"Therefore keep watch, because you do not know on what day your Lord will come." (Matthew 24:42)

After lambasting the religious leaders for their hypocrisy, Jesus continues his teaching, proclaiming what will happen in the future.

At first, it seems like a near-term prophecy that was fulfilled back in the first century, but as we continue reading Jesus's words, we see he's definitely talking about the end times. Perhaps the beginning of his future-focused words applied to the people then and have a secondary meaning for us later.

Regardless, he tells us to keep watch, steadfastly

looking for him. We don't know when he'll come back, but we better be ready. The angels don't know when this will happen, neither does he. Only his Father knows the date and time.

Jesus reminds us of Noah. The people continued living as usual, not knowing that disaster was about to befall them. They continued to focus on the present by eating and drinking. They continued to plan for the future by getting married.

They weren't ready, but Noah was. He and his family entered the ark, and the rains came. The earth flooded and carried all the unsuspecting people away—to their death. Only Noah and his family survived. Therefore, we must keep watch and be ready.

Consider two people working together. One is taken, and the other is left.

Jesus's next illustration to be diligent for his return is about a homeowner and a thief. If the owner knew when the thief would rob him, he'd be alert to guard against the burglary and keep his possessions safe.

Next is a servant who oversees his master's other servants. If the man feeds the servants and takes care of them, the master will return and affirm his worker's diligence. Yet if the servant isn't careful in his duties, mistreating the other servants and caring only for himself, the master will return to punish his unworthy helper.

These are all illustrations to remind us that Jesus could come back at any moment. Therefore, we must be watching for him. We must handle our assignments with care, lest we prove ourselves unworthy by not being ready when he returns.

We don't know when Jesus will come back, except that he will show up when we least expect him.

Are we looking for Jesus to return at any moment? What should we remove from our lives that keeps us from being ready when he comes back?

[Discover more about being ready in Luke 12:38–48.]

DAY 34: WELL DONE
MATTHEW 25:1–30

"His master replied, 'Well done, good and faithful servant!
You have been faithful with a few things; I will put you in
charge of many things. Come and share your master's
happiness!'" (Matthew 25:21)

Jesus continues his teaching about his return at the end of time. He gives a parable about ten virgins waiting for the bridegroom. They know he's on his way, and they go out to wait for him to join in the celebration. They take their lamps with them in case it's dark when he returns.

The bridegroom doesn't come back as soon as the girls expect. They get tired. Their eyelids are heavy. They soon drift off to sleep. At midnight, someone calls out that the bridegroom's arriving and urges the virgins to go meet him.

All ten wake up. With excitement, they trim their lamps so they have enough light to see in the dark. But the oil in their lamps is about gone. Five of the women had brought extra oil. The other five had not.

They beg the first five to share with them, but the wise virgins decline, for there will not be enough oil for them all. They encourage the five who didn't bring extra oil to hurry off and buy some. But while they're gone, the groom shows up. He goes into the celebration with the five wise virgins. The door shuts behind them.

When the other five return, with their lamps now shining brightly, they knock on the door. But they're denied entrance because they weren't there ready and waiting when the bridegroom arrived.

Therefore, we're to keep watch because we don't know when Jesus will come back.

The Teacher then shares another parable. It's about a man who prepares to leave on a long journey. He entrusts money to three of his servants.

The first receives five bags of gold. He uses the money wisely and earns five more bags. The second servant receives two bags of gold. He, too, acts wisely and earns two more bags. The third servant receives one bag of gold. He hides the gold to keep it safe.

After a long time away, the master returns and checks on his servants.

To the man who started with five bags and ended with ten, the master says, "Well done! You're a good and faithful servant. I'll put you in charge of many more things. Come, let's celebrate."

To the man who started with two bags and ended with four, the master gives the same response. "Well done! You're a good and faithful servant. I'll put you in charge of many more things. Come, let's celebrate."

To the man who could merely return his initial one bag of gold, the master says, "You wicked, lazy servant!" This third servant didn't even bother to deposit it to earn interest. The master takes away his bag of gold and gives it to another, kicking him out of the celebration.

Whatever God gives us, whether a little or a lot, whether money, possessions, or abilities, he expects us to make the most of it. We should use it wisely to grow his kingdom and not squander what he has blessed us with.

How well are we doing at using God's provisions to the best of our abilities? Is Jesus more apt to tell us well done or to call us wicked and lazy?

[Discover more about being a faithful servant in Psalm 85:8, Luke 19:11–27, and Hebrews 3:5.]

DAY 35: THE LEAST OF THESE
MATTHEW 25:31–46

"The King will reply, 'Truly I tell you, whatever you did for one of the least of these brothers and sisters of mine, you did for me.'" (Matthew 25:40)

I magine us hearing a knock on the door of our home. We look outside and there stands Jesus. He's hungry. He asks for food. What will we do? Since it's Jesus, we open our door wide and invite him in. We prepare a meal for him. Not just any meal, but the best we can make. Even if we have little to offer, we give whatever we have to him.

Or maybe Jesus is thirsty, needs a place to stay, or has nothing to wear. Perhaps he's sick, or we learn he's in prison. Would we help him? Of course we would!

We'd probably react much the same way if it was our minister, best friend, or family member who came knocking. But what if it was someone we didn't know? Would we invite a stranger in and offer whatever food we had? Maybe we'd shake our head and say we had nothing to spare. Maybe we'd judge them, and tell them to go get a job, slamming the door in their face.

Keep this in mind as we explore yet another teaching of Jesus about his return at the end of time. All people from all nations come before him. He separates them into two groups, just like a shepherd separating sheep from goats. He puts the sheep on his right and the goats on the left.

To the sheep—the people on his right—he says, "Come on in, my blessed ones. Receive your inheritance." Then he explains. "When I was hungry, you fed me. When I was thirsty, you gave me something to drink. When I was a stranger, you gave me shelter. When I needed something to wear, you clothed me. When I was sick, you took care of me. And when I was in prison, you visited me."

The people don't know what he's talking about. They don't remember helping Jesus in any of these situations. That's when he makes a shocking statement. "When you did it for others—even the least of all people—it was as though you were doing it for me."

Then Jesus turns to the goats—the people on his left—and sends them away. He curses them and condemns them to hell. Why? "Because I was hungry, but you gave me nothing to eat," he says. "I was thirsty, but you gave me nothing to drink. I was a stranger, but you didn't give me shelter. I needed something to wear, but you didn't clothe me. I was sick and in prison, but you ignored me."

These people don't know what he's talking about either. They have no recollection of Jesus being in need and them turning him away. That's when he explains. "When you failed to do it for others—even the least of all people—it was as though you failed me."

This passage is most convicting, revealing the importance of helping others when they struggle. Yet we must be careful to not overreact and conclude that we need to earn our salvation (Ephesians 2:8–9). That would be an overreach.

The central point of Jesus's teaching is that we help those in need and don't dismiss their plight.

In what ways can we better help people during their times of need? Though we can't earn our salvation, what should we do in response to the salvation Jesus freely gives us?

[Discover more about helping others in James 2:14–26.]

DAY 36: PASSOVER
MATTHEW 26:1–30

While they were eating, Jesus took bread, and when he had given thanks, he broke it and gave it to his disciples, saying, "Take and eat; this is my body." (Matthew 26:26)

In the book of Exodus, we read about God's chosen people enslaved in Egypt. Through Moses he's orchestrating his plan so his people can flee their captors. It's their exodus from slavery, hence the name of the book.

God has already sent nine plagues to get Pharaoh's attention and bring about the Hebrew people's release. This will culminate with the tenth plague, the worst of them all. In this plague, the first-born male of every family, as well as of all animals, will die.

Yet God gives his people a way to protect themselves. They're to sacrifice a lamb, eat it in celebration with family, according to his instructions, and brush its blood on their home's doorframe. When God comes at midnight to kill the firstborn, he'll pass over every house marked with blood.

They're to repeat this ceremony annually in remembrance of God's provision when he passed over them. For this reason, they call the celebration Passover (Exodus 11–12).

Fast forward to Jesus. It's time for the annual Passover observance and he wishes to celebrate it with his disciples. They gather to remember what God did many centuries before as they eat the meal.

During their Passover remembrance, Jesus takes the bread, thanks God for it, and divides it. He gives some to each disciple. "Take it and eat. This is my body."

Next, he raises a cup of wine. He gives thanks for it and shares it with them. "Drink from the cup, everyone. This is the blood of my covenant, poured out as an offering for the forgiveness of sins."

In doing so, Jesus extends the Passover celebration to become Communion, also known as the

Lord's Supper or the Eucharist. What began as a sacrificial lamb to save the first-born male of every family changes to become Jesus's sacrifice to save everyone. In this way, Passover grows to become Communion. Jesus gives a new meaning to this revered ritual, which now takes on a fresh significance for all who follow Jesus.

When we repeat this ritual in our practices today, we remember Jesus and what he did for us—or at least we should.

What should communion mean to us today? Does it serve as a reminder of what Jesus did for us when he died to save us from our sins?

[Discover more about the Lord's Supper in Mark 14:12–26, Luke 22:7–23, and 1 Corinthians 11:17–34.]

DAY 37: NOT MY WILL
MATTHEW 26:31–46

Going a little farther, he fell with his face to the ground and prayed, "My Father, if it is possible, may this cup be taken from me. Yet not as I will, but as you will." (Matthew 26:39)

After Jesus expands the meaning of Passover into being a celebration of his sacrifice for us, he and his disciples go to Gethsemane. Leaving the other nine to wait, he takes Peter, James, and John. They follow Jesus as he goes to pray. He's overwhelmed with sorrow by the task before him. He asks for their support as he talks to his Father.

Jesus implores God to take away the burden of

his upcoming sacrificial death. Yet Jesus confirms he'll do whatever Papa wants.

After revealing his heart's desire to his Father, he returns to his disciples, who were supposed to support him and keep vigil. Yet he finds them asleep. Rousing them and encouraging them to persevere, he prays to Father God a second time.

Again, he returns to find his three disciples sleeping. He leaves them to their slumber, while he prays the same request a third time.

His honest prayer, offered three times, reveals his innermost thoughts. He prefers not to die, but he will follow through if that's what his Father wants. Does this suggest he questions his mission? Does this imply he wants to give up?

No. This doesn't mean Jesus has second thoughts. He's likely thinking of the story of Abraham when God tells the patriarch to offer his son, Isaac, as a sacrifice. Abraham intends to do just that, obeying what God commanded.

With the altar built and the wood for the sacrificial fire lying upon it, Abraham binds Isaac and places him on top of it. Abraham raises his dagger and prepares to kill his son, but God stops him. He draws his servant's attention to a ram caught in a thicket.

The ram becomes a substitute offering in place of Isaac, sparing Abraham the agony of killing his son. It was just a test of his faith and obedience. Abraham passes, and Isaac lives (Genesis 22:1–19).

Though it's only speculation, it's easy to see Jesus recalling this story of God reverting to Plan B for Isaac. Does God have a Plan B for Jesus? Is it only a test?

No. This time it is not a test. There is no Plan B. Jesus must die as the ultimate sacrifice for the people's sins. There's no other way to produce a permanent solution to absolve the people of their disobedience.

God will sacrifice his only Son. Jesus will die, but all those who believe in him will live.

When have we last thanked Jesus for dying to save us? When we don't want to do what God tells us to do, are we still willing to obey?

[Discover two other times Jesus focused on Peter, James, and John in Matthew 17:1–9 and Mark 5:35–43. Read about when Paul makes a threefold request to God in 2 Corinthians 12:8–9.]

DAY 38: I DON'T KNOW HIM
MATTHEW 26:47–75

Then [Peter] began to call down curses, and he swore to them, "I don't know the man!" Immediately a rooster crowed.
(Matthew 26:74)

O f Jesus's twelve disciples, Peter's name appears more often in the book of Matthew than the other eleven. This shows him as the emerging leader of the group, as well as giving credence to him as a man who is quick to act and swift to speak.

In "Day 20: Walk on Water," we see Peter as the only disciple who leaves the safety of the boat to walk on water. Though his miraculous journey is short, he's the lone disciple to try. Aside from Jesus,

Peter is the only person to accomplish this amazing feat (Matthew 14:22–33).

Next, in "Day 23: Peter's Testimony," we see Peter as the first one to answer Jesus's pointed question of "Who do you say that I am?" The disciple's response is both quick and profound. "You are the Messiah, the Son of God." Jesus affirms Peter and his astute answer (Matthew 16:15-17).

Third, when Jesus institutes the celebration of Communion and predicts that Judas will betray him, Jesus adds that they'll all fall away. But Peter claims he won't. He boldly states that even if everyone else abandons Jesus, he never will. He's even willing to die for Jesus. That's when the Savior predicts that before the rooster crows, Peter will three times deny even knowing him (Matthew 26:33–35).

I applaud Peter for his confidence, and I'm quick to join him in saying that I'd never deny Jesus. Yet these are easy pledges to make when we don't face pressure, when we feel safe.

Only a few hours later, Judas betrays his Lord, and Jesus is arrested. They drag the Savior before the Sanhedrin and conduct a mock trial. Peter waits outside in the courtyard. There, a servant girl identifies him as someone who was with Jesus. He denies it, saying, "I have no idea what you're talking about."

He walks away and moves to the courtyard entrance. Another servant girl likewise points him out as someone who was with Jesus. This time Peter's response is more adamant. "I don't even know the man!"

Yet Peter can't escape their scrutiny. Others claim that his accent gives him away. Peter calls down curses on himself before swearing that he doesn't know Jesus.

Then the rooster crows.

Peter remembers Jesus's prediction and slinks away in shame to shed bitter tears of remorse.

Yet this isn't the end of Peter's story. Despite his momentary lapse, Jesus will later restore him, and he will lead Jesus's church.

When have we not spoken out for Jesus when we should have? When we falter, do we trust he will restore us?

[Discover Jesus restoring Peter in John 21:15–19.]

DAY 39: DIRECT ACCESS
MATTHEW 27

At that moment the curtain of the temple was torn in two from top to bottom. The earth shook, the rocks split and the tombs broke open. The bodies of many holy people who had died were raised to life. (Matthew 27:51–52)

Taking place while Peter denies he knows Jesus, the religious leaders conduct an unfair trial of the Teacher. They already know the outcome will be Jesus's execution, but they need to first fabricate testimony to support their pre-determined conclusion.

The Jews have only limited autonomy given to them by their Roman occupiers. They don't have the authority to execute anyone, so they need Rome to do it. The religious leaders manipulate Pilate, and they manipulate the people. At last, Pilate relents and sanctions Jesus's crucifixion. The Roman soldiers follow through, mocking and abusing him as they prepare to execute him.

Hanging on the cross in agony, Jesus's death marches closer. He cries out and dies. His sacrifice is complete, but it's not the end. It's also the beginning—for all of us.

With his passing, the curtain in the temple rips in two from top to bottom. The earth shakes, rocks split, and tombs open. Many holy people resurrect from their graves.

This fills us with awe, and we can join with the centurion and soldiers in saying, "Truly, he was the Son of God."

Let's focus, however, on the curtain in the temple being torn in two.

First, this would be the curtain that separates the Holy Place from the Most Holy Place (Exodus 26:33). The people viewed the Most Holy Place as God's dwelling here on earth. The curtain that separates it from the Holy Place (and the rest of the temple) serves symbolically to prohibit our access to God.

Only a priest could enter the Most Holy Place

and then only once a year. This one priest could approach God. No one else could enter God's presence.

Next, the curtain tore not from bottom to top, which would be the case if its rending was of human origin. Instead, it tore from top to bottom, revealing its rending as originating from above, as coming from God himself. In this way, we see Father God removing the barrier between him and us. This begins with Jesus's death as a human sacrifice to save us from all the wrong things we have done—and will do.

Not only does Jesus save us. In doing so, he gives us direct access to the Father. We now no longer need an intermediary to approach God. We can come to him anytime we want and for any reason.

What do we think about being able to approach God directly? In what ways do we still rely on an intermediary to function between us and our Heavenly Father?

[Discover more about this curtain and its significance in Hebrews 6:19–20, Hebrews 9, and Hebrews 10:19–25.]

BONUS CONTENT: MATTHEW REFERENCES THE OLD TESTAMENT

Then what was spoken by Jeremiah the prophet was fulfilled: "They took the thirty pieces of silver, the price set on him by the people of Israel, and they used them to buy the potter's field, as the Lord commanded me." (Matthew 27:9–10)

Aside from the book of Romans, Matthew makes more Old Testament references than any other book of the Bible. There are fifty such instances where he either quotes from the Old Testament or references it.

Here is the list:

- Matthew 1:23 fulfills Isaiah 7:14

- Matthew 2:6 comes from Micah 5:2 and 4
- Matthew 2:15 quotes Hosea 11:1
- Matthew 2:18 references Jeremiah 31:15
- Matthew 3:3 fulfills Isaiah 40:3
- Matthew 4:4 quotes Deuteronomy 8:3
- Matthew 4:6 quotes Psalm 91:11–12
- Matthew 4:7 quotes Deuteronomy 6:16
- Matthew 4:10 references Deuteronomy 6:13
- Matthew 4:16 comes from Isaiah 9:1–2
- Matthew 5:21 quotes Exodus 20:13
- Matthew 5:27 quotes Exodus 20:14
- Matthew 5:31 comes from Deuteronomy 24:1
- Matthew 5:38 is found in Exodus 21:24, Leviticus 24:20, and Deuteronomy 19:21
- Matthew 5:43 comes from Leviticus 19:18
- Matthew 8:17 fulfills Isaiah 53:4
- Matthew 9:13 quotes Hosea 6:6
- Matthew 10:36 refers to Micah 7:6
- Matthew 11:10 quotes Malachi 3:1
- Matthew 12:7 quotes Hosea 6:6

- Matthew 12:21 comes from Isaiah 42:1–4
- Matthew 13:15 refers to Isaiah 6:9–10
- Matthew 13:35 quotes Psalm 78:2
- Matthew 15:4 comes from Exodus 20:12 and Deuteronomy 5:16
- Matthew 15:4 also comes from Exodus 21:17 and Leviticus 20:9
- Matthew 15:9 refers to Isaiah 29:13
- Matthew 18:16 is based on Deuteronomy 19:15
- Matthew 19:4 quotes Genesis 1:27
- Matthew 19:5 quotes Genesis 2:24
- Matthew 19:19 refers to Exodus 20:12–16 and Deuteronomy 5:16–20
- Matthew 19:19 also refers to Leviticus 19:18
- Matthew 21:5 fulfills Zechariah 9:9
- Matthew 21:9 fulfills Psalm 118:25–26
- Matthew 21:13 refers to Isaiah 56:7 and Jeremiah 7:11
- Matthew 21:16 comes from Psalm 8:2
- Matthew 21:42 quotes Psalm 118:22–23
- Matthew 22:32 quotes Exodus 3:6
- Matthew 22:37 quotes Deuteronomy 6:5
- Matthew 22:39 quotes Leviticus 19:18

- Matthew 22:44 quotes Psalm 110:1
- Matthew 23:39 quotes Psalm 118:26
- Matthew 24:15 quotes from Daniel 9:27, 11:31, and 12:11
- Matthew 24:29 quotes from Isaiah 13:10 and 34:4
- Matthew 24:30 comes from Daniel 7:13–14
- Matthew 26:11 refers to Deuteronomy 15:11
- Matthew 26:31 fulfills Zechariah 13:7
- Matthew 26:64 comes from Psalm 110:1 and Daniel 7:13
- Matthew 27:10 fulfills Zechariah 11:12–13 and Jeremiah 19:1–13 and 32:6–9
- Matthew 27:46 fulfills Psalm 22:1

What do Matthew's many Old Testament references tell us about his account of Jesus? Which one of these Old Testament connections is the most surprising?

[Discover more about relating the Old Testament with the New Testament in Matthew 26:54.]

DAY 40: GO
MATTHEW 28

"Therefore go and make disciples of all nations, baptizing them in the name of the Father and of the Son and of the Holy Spirit, and teaching them to obey everything I have commanded you." (Matthew 28:19–20)

The story of Jesus's sacrifice to make us right with Father God doesn't end with his death. Nor does it end with his burial. Instead, his story continues. A few days later, Jesus rises from the grave. He overcomes death, proving his mastery over it.

Yet he doesn't intend to stay on earth in his resurrected form to lead his disciples. Instead, he will return to heaven and send them the Holy

Spirit. It's the Holy Spirit who will lead his disciples to grow Jesus's following.

Before the Savior returns to heaven, however, he gives his followers his final instructions. Matthew concludes his biography of Jesus with this as his last teaching to his followers.

We often call this the Great Commission. In this, he commissions his disciples for ministry, the greatest ministry they could ever pursue.

He tells them to go and make disciples. It's that simple. Where are they to go? It's not a message just for the Jews, God's chosen people. Instead, they're to go to all nations. That's everywhere and includes everyone. Salvation isn't just for the Jews. It's for the Gentiles as well. This means it's for you and me too.

As the disciples go and make disciples, there are two parts to their mission.

First, they need to baptize people in the name of the Father, Son, and Holy Spirit. Baptism is a public display of the people's commitment to follow Jesus. It extends the Old Testament ceremonial washing to make the priests clean. Though baptism doesn't actually wash our sins away, it shows we're clean through Jesus.

Symbolically, baptism—going into the water and emerging from it—gives us a visual reminder of

Jesus's death, burial, and resurrection. It's a beautiful rite.

The second part of making disciples is to teach the people everything about Jesus and to obey his instructions. We know what Jesus taught and commanded through Matthew's record of his life, along with the books of Mark, Luke, and John. Through these accounts, we can learn about Jesus and what he told us to do.

Then we must obey everything he said.

What can we do to go and make disciples? As we teach others to obey Jesus's commands, how can we better serve as an example?

[Discover more about Jesus's last instructions in Mark 16:15–18 and Acts 1:4–9.]

If you liked *Matthew Bible Study,* please leave a review online. Your review will help others discover this book and encourage them to read it too.

Thank you.

BOOKS IN THE 40-DAY BIBLE STUDY SERIES

Which book do you want to read next in the 40-Day Bible Study Series?

- Dear Theophilus (the Gospel of **Luke**, formerly That You May Know)
- Dear Theophilus, **Acts** (formerly Tongues of Fire)
- Dear Theophilus, **Isaiah** (formerly For Unto Us)
- Dear Theophilus, **Minor Prophets** (formerly Return to Me)
- Dear Theophilus, **Job** (formerly I Hope in Him)
- Living Water (**John**)

FOR SMALL GROUPS, SUNDAY SCHOOL, AND CLASSES

Matthew Bible Study makes an ideal eight-week Bible study discussion guide for small groups, Sunday school, and classes. To prepare for the conversation, read one chapter of this book each weekday, Monday through Friday.

- Week 1: read 1 through 5.
- Week 2: read 6 through 10.
- Week 3: read 11 through 15.
- Week 4: read 16 through 20.
- Week 5: read 21 through 25.
- Week 6: read 26 through 30.
- Week 7: read 31 through 35.
- Week 8: read 36 through 40.

When you get together, discuss the questions at the end of each chapter. The leader can use all the questions to guide your discussion or pick which ones to focus on.

Before you begin, pray as a group. Ask for Holy Spirit insight and clarity.

As you consider each chapter's questions:

- Look for how this can grow your understanding of the Bible.
- Evaluate how this can expand your faith perspective.
- Consider what you need to change in how you live your lives.

End by asking God to help you apply what you've learned.

May God bless you as you read and study his Word.

IF YOU'RE NEW TO THE BIBLE

Each entry in this book contains Bible references. These can guide you if you want to learn more. If you're not familiar with the Bible, here's an overview to get you started, give some context, and minimize confusion.

First, the Bible is a collection of works written by various authors over several centuries. Think of the Bible as a diverse anthology of godly communication. It contains historical accounts, poetry, songs, letters of instruction and encouragement, messages from God sent through his representatives, and prophecies.

Most versions of the Bible have sixty-six books grouped into two sections: The Old Testament and the New Testament. The Old Testament contains thirty-nine books that precede and anticipate Jesus. The New Testament includes twenty-seven books and covers Jesus's life and the work of his followers.

The reference notations in the Bible, such as Romans 3:23, are analogous to line numbers in a Shakespearean play. They serve as a study aid. Since the Bible is much longer and more complex than a play, its reference notations are more involved.

As already mentioned, the Bible is an amalgam of books, or sections, such as Genesis, Psalms, or Matthew. These are the names given to them, over time, based on the piece's author, audience, or purpose.

In the 1200s, each book was divided into chapters, such as Acts 2 or Psalm 23. In the 1500s, the chapters were further subdivided into verses, such as John 3:16. Let's use this as an example.

The name of the book (John) appears first, followed by the chapter number (3), a colon, and then the verse number (16). Sometimes called a chapter-verse reference notation, this helps people quickly find a specific text regardless of their version of the Bible.

Although the goal was to place these chapter and verse divisions at logical breaks, they sometimes seem arbitrary. Therefore, it's good practice to read what precedes and follows each passage you're studying. The text before or after it may contain relevant insights into the portion you're exploring.

Here's how to look up a specific passage in the Bible based on its reference: Most Bibles contain a table of contents, which gives the page number for the beginning of each book. Start there. Locate the book you want to read, and turn to that page. Then flip forward to the chapter you want. Last, skim that chapter to locate the specific verse.

If you want to read online, enter the reference into BibleGateway.com or BibleHub.com. Also check out the YouVersion app.

Learn more about the greatest book ever written at ABibleADay.com, which provides a Bible blog, summaries of the books of the Bible, a dictionary of Bible terms, Bible reading plans, and other resources.

ABOUT PETER DEHAAN

Peter DeHaan, PhD, wants to change the world one word at a time. His books and blog posts discuss God, the Bible, and church, geared toward spiritual seekers and church dropouts. Many people feel church has let them down, and Peter seeks to encourage them as they search for a place to belong.

But he's not afraid to ask tough questions or make religious people squirm. He's not trying to be provocative. Instead, he seeks truth, even if it makes people uncomfortable. Peter urges Christians to push past the status quo and reexamine how they practice their faith in every part of their lives.

Peter earned his doctorate, awarded with high distinction, from Trinity College of the Bible and Theological Seminary. He lives with his wife in beautiful Southwest Michigan and wrangles crossword puzzles in his spare time.

A lifelong student of Scripture, Peter wrote the 1,000-page website ABibleADay.com to encourage people to explore the Bible, the greatest book ever written. His popular blog, at PeterDeHaan.com, addresses biblical Christianity to build a faith that matters.

Read his blog, receive his newsletter, and learn more at PeterDeHaan.com.

BOOKS BY PETER DEHAAN

40-Day Bible Study Series

Dear Theophilus (the Gospel of Luke, formerly That You May Know)

Dear Theophilus, Acts (formerly Tongues of Fire)

Dear Theophilus, Isaiah (formerly For Unto Us)

Dear Theophilus, Minor Prophets (formerly Return to Me)

Dear Theophilus, Job (formerly I Hope in Him)

Living Water (the Gospel of John)

Love Is Patient (Paul's letters to the Corinthians)

Revelation Bible Study

Love One Another (John's letters)

Run with Perseverance (the book of Hebrews)

James and Jude Bible Study

Holiday Celebration Series

The Advent of Jesus (an Advent devotional)

The Passion of Jesus (a Lenten devotional)

The Victory of Jesus (an Easter devotional)

The Ministry of Jesus (an Ordinary Time devotional)

Bible Character Sketches Series

Women of the Bible

The Friends and Foes of Jesus

Old Testament Sinners and Saints

More Old Testament Sinners and Saints

Heroes and Heavies of the Apocrypha

200 Old Testament Sinners and Saints

Visiting Churches Series

Shopping for Church

Visiting Online Church

52 Churches

The 52 Churches Workbook

More Than 52 Churches

The More Than 52 Churches Workbook

Other Books

Jesus's Broken Church

Martin Luther's 95 Theses

The Christian Church's LGBTQ Failure

Bridging the Sacred-Secular Divide

Beyond Psalm 150

How Big Is Your Tent?

For the latest list of all Peter's books, go to
PeterDeHaan.com/books.